CONTENTS

Modify XML with ElementTree in Python

Validate XML with lxml in Python

Perform XPath queries in Python using lxml

Parse and generate XML using JavaScript (DOM)

Parse XML using JavaScript (SAX)

Read and write XML files in C#

Validate XML in C#

Use LINQ to XML in C#

Parse XML in Perl using XML::LibXML module

Use XML::Simple module for XML parsing in Perl

Parse and manipulate XML in PHP

Generate XML from database queries in PHP

Implement XML-RPC client and server in Python

Implement SOAP (Simple Object Access Protocol) web services

Create RSS feeds in XML format

Parse Atom feeds using XML

Parse SVG (Scalable Vector Graphics) with XML

Transform XML using XSL-FO (XSL Formatting Objects)

Use XML for configuration files in software development

Parse XML responses from APIs in Android applications

Use XML layout files in Android development

Parse XML configuration files in Spring Framework

Use XML for messaging with JMS (Java Messaging Service)

Implement XML data binding in .NET

Serialize and deserialize XML in .NET

Use XPath queries in .NET

Use XQuery to query XML data

Implement XQuery expressions and functions

Use XML for creating multimedia presentations (SMIL)

Implement XML for representing business processes (BPEL)

Use XML for representing vector graphics (SVG)

Implement XML for representing mathematical formulas (MathML)

Use XML for representing chemical structures (CML)

Implement XML for representing user interface layouts (XUL)

Use XML for representing syndicated content (RSS, Atom)

Implement XML for representing user profiles (XUP)

Use XML for representing geospatial data (GML)

Implement XML for representing calendar data (iCalendar)

Use XML for representing 3D graphics (X3D)

Implement XML for representing genealogical data (GEDCOM)

Use XML for representing electronic books (ePub)

Implement XML for representing bibliographic references (MODS)

Use XML for representing chemical data (CDXML)

Implement XML for representing music scores (MusicXML)

Use XML for representing statistical data (SDMX)

Implement XML for representing electronic health records (CDA)

Use XML for representing legal documents (LegalXML)

Implement XML for representing educational content (SCORM)

Use XML for representing financial transactions (OFX)

Implement XML for representing project management data (MPX)

Use XML for representing structured documents (DocBook)

Implement XML for representing syndicated web content (RDF)

Use XML for representing remote procedure calls (XML-RPC)

Implement XML for representing mathematical markup (MathML)

Use XML for representing chemical data (CML)

Implement XML for representing GIS data (GML)

Use XML for representing e-commerce transactions (UBL)

Implement XML for representing multimedia presentations (SMIL)

Use XML for representing user interfaces (XUL)

Implement XML for representing digital books (EPUB)

Use XML for representing bibliographic information (MODS)

Implement XML for representing news syndication (RSS/ATOM)

Use XML for representing genealogy data (GEDCOM)

Implement XML for representing multimedia content (SVG)

Use XML for representing mathematical formulas (MathML)

Implement XML for representing geographic data (GML)

Use XML for representing legal documents (LegalXML)

Implement XML for representing educational content (SCORM)

Use XML for representing financial data (XBRL)

Implement XML for representing project data (MPX)

Use XML for representing web services (WSDL)

Implement XML for representing business processes (BPEL)

Use XML for representing healthcare data (CDA)

Implement XML for representing office documents (OpenXML)

Use XML for representing electronic books (EPUB)

Implement XML for representing bibliographic data (MARC)

Use XML for representing calendar data (iCalendar)

Implement XML for representing metadata (Dublin Core)

Use XML for representing social network data (FOAF)

Implement XML for representing e-learning content (SCORM)

Use XML for representing financial transactions (OFX)

Implement XML for representing project management data (MPX)

Use XML for representing structured documents (DocBook)

Implement XML for representing syndicated web content (RDF)

Use XML for representing remote procedure calls (XML-RPC)

Implement XML for representing mathematical markup (MathML)

Use XML for representing chemical data (CML)

Implement XML for representing GIS data (GML)

Use XML for representing e-commerce transactions (UBL)

Implement XML for representing multimedia presentations (SMIL)

Use XML for representing user interfaces (XUL)

Implement XML for representing digital books (EPUB)

Use XML for representing bibliographic information (MODS)

Implement XML for representing news syndication (RSS/ATOM)

Use XML for representing genealogy data (GEDCOM)

Implement XML for representing multimedia content (SVG)

Use XML for representing mathematical formulas (MathML)

Implement XML for representing geographic data (GML)

Use XML for representing legal documents (LegalXML)

Implement XML for representing educational content (SCORM)

Use XML for representing financial data (XBRL)

Implement XML for representing project data (MPX)

Use XML for representing web services (WSDL)

Implement XML for representing business processes (BPEL)

Use XML for representing healthcare data (CDA)

Implement XML for representing office documents (OpenXML)

Use XML for representing electronic books (EPUB)

Implement XML for representing bibliographic data (MARC)

Use XML for representing calendar data (iCalendar)

Implement XML for representing metadata (Dublin Core)

Use XML for representing social network data (FOAF)

Implement XML for representing e-learning content (SCORM)

Use XML for representing financial transactions (OFX)

Implement XML for representing project management data (MPX)

Use XML for representing structured documents (DocBook)

Implement XML for representing syndicated web content (RDF)

Use XML for representing remote procedure calls (XML-RPC)

Implement XML for representing mathematical markup (MathML)

Use XML for representing chemical data (CML)

Implement XML for representing GIS data (GML)

Use XML for representing e-commerce transactions (UBL)

Implement XML for representing multimedia presentations (SMIL)

Use XML for representing user interfaces (XUL)

Implement XML for representing digital books (EPUB)

Use XML for representing bibliographic information (MODS)

Implement XML for representing news syndication (RSS/ATOM)

Use XML for representing genealogy data (GEDCOM)

Implement XML for representing multimedia content (SVG)

Use XML for representing mathematical formulas (MathML)

Implement XML for representing geographic data (GML)

Use XML for representing legal documents (LegalXML)

Implement XML for representing educational content (SCORM)

Use XML for representing financial data (XBRL)

Implement XML for representing project data (MPX)

Use XML for representing web services (WSDL)

Implement XML for representing business processes (BPEL)

Use XML for representing healthcare data (CDA)

Implement XML for representing office documents (OpenXML)

Use XML for representing electronic books (EPUB)

Implement XML for representing bibliographic data (MARC)

Use XML for representing calendar data (iCalendar)

Implement XML for representing metadata (Dublin Core)

Use XML for representing social network data (FOAF)

Implement XML for representing e-learning content (SCORM)

Use XML for representing financial transactions (OFX)

Implement XML for representing project management data (MPX)

Use XML for representing structured documents (DocBook)

Implement XML for representing syndicated web content (RDF)

Use XML for representing remote procedure calls (XML-RPC)

Implement XML for representing mathematical markup (MathML)

Use XML for representing chemical data (CML)

Implement XML for representing GIS data (GML)

Use XML for representing e-commerce transactions (UBL)

Implement XML for representing multimedia presentations (SMIL)

Use XML for representing user interfaces (XUL)

Implement XML for representing digital books (EPUB)

Use XML for representing bibliographic information (MODS)

Implement XML for representing news syndication (RSS/ATOM)

Use XML for representing genealogy data (GEDCOM)

Implement XML for representing multimedia content (SVG)

Use XML for representing mathematical formulas (MathML)

Implement XML for representing geographic data (GML)

Use XML for representing legal documents (LegalXML)

Implement XML for representing educational content (SCORM)

Use XML for representing financial data (XBRL)

Implement XML for representing project data (MPX)

Use XML for representing web services (WSDL)

Implement XML for representing business processes (BPEL)

CONTENTS

Creating a Simple XML Document

```xml
<?xml version="1.0" encoding="UTF-8"?>
<bookstore>
  <book>
    <title>Harry Potter and the Philosopher's Stone</title>
    <author>J.K. Rowling</author>
    <genre>Fantasy</genre>
    <price>19.99</price>
  </book>
  <book>
    <title>The Hobbit</title>
    <author>J.R.R. Tolkien</author>
    <genre>Fantasy</genre>
    <price>14.99</price>
  </book>
</bookstore>
```

Adding Elements and Attributes to an XML Document

```xml
<?xml version="1.0" encoding="UTF-8"?>
<employee>
  <name first="John" last="Doe"/>
  <department id="101">
    <role>Manager</role>
    <location>New York</location>
  </department>
</employee>
```

Creating Nested Elements in XML

```xml
<?xml version="1.0" encoding="UTF-8"?>
<menu>
```

```
  <category name="Appetizers">

    <item>Salad</item>

    <item>Spring Rolls</item>

  </category>

  <category name="Main Course">

    <item>Steak</item>

    <item>Pasta</item>

  </category>

</menu>
```

Using XML Comments

```
<?xml version="1.0" encoding="UTF-8"?>

<config>

  <!-- This is a sample configuration file -->

  <server>

    <hostname>example.com</hostname>

    <port>8080</port>

  </server>

</config>
```

Defining XML Namespaces

```
<?xml version="1.0" encoding="UTF-8"?>

<root xmlns:ns1="http://example.com/ns1">

  <ns1:element>Content</ns1:element>

</root>
```

Validating XML Against a DTD (Document Type Definition)

```
<?xml version="1.0"?>

<!DOCTYPE note SYSTEM "note.dtd">

<note>

  <to>Tove</to>
```

```
  <from>Jani</from>
  <heading>Reminder</heading>
  <body>Don't forget me this weekend!</body>
</note>
```

Validating XML Against an XSD (XML Schema Definition)

```
<?xml version="1.0"?>
<book xmlns:xsi="http://www.w3.org/2001/XMLSchema-instance"
   xsi:noNamespaceSchemaLocation="book.xsd">
  <title>Java Programming</title>
  <author>John Doe</author>
  <price>29.99</price>
</book>
```

Using XPath to Select XML Nodes

```
<?xml version="1.0" encoding="UTF-8"?>
<library>
  <book>
    <title>Harry Potter and the Philosopher's Stone</title>
    <author>J.K. Rowling</author>
    <genre>Fantasy</genre>
    <price>19.99</price>
  </book>
  <book>
    <title>The Hobbit</title>
    <author>J.R.R. Tolkien</author>
    <genre>Fantasy</genre>
    <price>14.99</price>
  </book>
  <magazine>
    <title>National Geographic</title>
```

```
    <issue>April 2024</issue>
  </magazine>
</library>
```

XPath to select all book titles:

```
/library/book/title
```

Using XPath to Select Attributes

```
<?xml version="1.0" encoding="UTF-8"?>
<employees>
  <employee id="101">
    <name>John Doe</name>
    <position>Manager</position>
    <salary>50000</salary>
  </employee>
  <employee id="102">
    <name>Jane Smith</name>
    <position>Developer</position>
    <salary>40000</salary>
  </employee>
</employees>
```

XPath to select the id attribute of all employees:

```
/employees/employee/@id
```

Using XPath to Navigate XML Tree Structure

```
<?xml version="1.0" encoding="UTF-8"?>
<catalog>
  <book>
    <title>JavaScript: The Good Parts</title>
    <author>Douglas Crockford</author>
    <price>29.99</price>
  </book>
```

```
  <book>
    <title>Head First Design Patterns</title>
    <author>Eric Freeman</author>
    <price>39.99</price>
  </book>
</catalog>
```

XPath to navigate to the price of the second book:

/catalog/book[2]/price

Using XPath Functions (string, number, boolean)

```
<?xml version="1.0" encoding="UTF-8"?>
<students>
  <student>
    <name>John Doe</name>
    <age>20</age>
    <grade>A</grade>
  </student>
  <student>
    <name>Jane Smith</name>
    <age>22</age>
    <grade>B+</grade>
  </student>
</students>
```

XPath to convert age to a number and check if it's greater than 21:

number(/students/student[2]/age) > 21

Using XPath Axes (child, parent, descendant, ancestor)

```
<?xml version="1.0" encoding="UTF-8"?>
<library>
  <book>
    <title>Harry Potter and the Philosopher's Stone</title>
```

```xml
    <author>J.K. Rowling</author>
    <genre>Fantasy</genre>
    <price>19.99</price>
  </book>
  <book>
    <title>The Hobbit</title>
    <author>J.R.R. Tolkien</author>
    <genre>Fantasy</genre>
    <price>14.99</price>
  </book>
  <magazine>
    <title>National Geographic</title>
    <issue>April 2024</issue>
  </magazine>
</library>
```

XPath to select all child elements of the library node:

/library/*

XPath to select all ancestor elements of the title node:

/title/ancestor::*

Using XPath Predicates for Filtering

```xml
<?xml version="1.0" encoding="UTF-8"?>
<employees>
  <employee>
    <name>John Doe</name>
    <position>Manager</position>
    <salary>50000</salary>
  </employee>
  <employee>
    <name>Jane Smith</name>
    <position>Developer</position>
```

```xml
    <salary>40000</salary>
  </employee>
</employees>
```

XPath to filter employees based on salary greater than 45000:

```
/employees/employee[salary > 45000]
```

Implementing XSLT Transformation to Convert XML to HTML

```xml
<?xml version="1.0" encoding="UTF-8"?>
<xsl:stylesheet version="1.0" xmlns:xsl="http://www.w3.org/1999/XSL/Transform">
  <xsl:template match="/">
    <html>
      <body>
        <h1>Employee List</h1>
        <ul>
          <xsl:for-each select="employees/employee">
            <li><xsl:value-of select="name"/> - <xsl:value-of select="position"/></li>
          </xsl:for-each>
        </ul>
      </body>
    </html>
  </xsl:template>
</xsl:stylesheet>
```

Implementing XSLT Transformation to Convert XML to Another XML Format

```xml
<?xml version="1.0" encoding="UTF-8"?>
<xsl:stylesheet version="1.0" xmlns:xsl="http://www.w3.org/1999/XSL/Transform">
  <xsl:template match="/">
    <newformat>
      <xsl:apply-templates select="library/book"/>
    </newformat>
```

```
  </xsl:template>

    <xsl:template match="book">

    <book>

      <title><xsl:value-of select="title"/></title>

      <author><xsl:value-of select="author"/></author>

    </book>

  </xsl:template>

</xsl:stylesheet>
```

Using XSLT for Conditional Processing (if-else)

```
<?xml version="1.0" encoding="UTF-8"?>

<xsl:stylesheet version="1.0" xmlns:xsl="http://www.w3.org/1999/XSL/Transform">

  <xsl:template match="/">

    <html>

      <body>

        <xsl:choose>

          <xsl:when test="library/book/genre = 'Fantasy'">

            <h1>Fantasy Books</h1>

          </xsl:when>

          <xsl:otherwise>

            <h1>Other Genre Books</h1>

          </xsl:otherwise>

        </xsl:choose>

      </body>

    </html>

  </xsl:template>

</xsl:stylesheet>
```

Using XSLT for Looping (for-each)

```
<?xml version="1.0" encoding="UTF-8"?>

<xsl:stylesheet version="1.0" xmlns:xsl="http://www.w3.org/1999/XSL/Transform">
```

```
<xsl:template match="/">
  <html>
    <body>
      <h1>Employee List</h1>
      <ul>
        <xsl:for-each select="employees/employee">
          <li><xsl:value-of select="name"/> - <xsl:value-of select="position"/></li>
        </xsl:for-each>
      </ul>
    </body>
  </html>
</xsl:template>
</xsl:stylesheet>
```

Using XSLT Templates

```
<?xml version="1.0" encoding="UTF-8"?>
<xsl:stylesheet version="1.0" xmlns:xsl="http://www.w3.org/1999/XSL/Transform">
  <xsl:template match="/">
    <html>
      <body>
        <xsl:apply-templates select="catalog/book"/>
      </body>
    </html>
  </xsl:template>

  <xsl:template match="book">
    <div>
      <h2><xsl:value-of select="title"/></h2>
      <p>Author: <xsl:value-of select="author"/></p>
      <p>Price: <xsl:value-of select="price"/></p>
```

```
      </div>
  </xsl:template>
</xsl:stylesheet>
```

Using XSLT Sorting and Grouping

```
<?xml version="1.0" encoding="UTF-8"?>
<xsl:stylesheet version="1.0" xmlns:xsl="http://www.w3.org/1999/XSL/Transform">
  <xsl:template match="/">
    <html>
      <body>
        <h1>Books by Genre</h1>
        <xsl:for-each select="library/book">
          <xsl:sort select="genre"/>
          <xsl:if test="position() = 1 or genre != preceding-sibling::book[1]/genre">
            <h2><xsl:value-of select="genre"/></h2>
          </xsl:if>
          <p><xsl:value-of select="title"/> - <xsl:value-of select="author"/></p>
        </xsl:for-each>
      </body>
    </html>
  </xsl:template>
</xsl:stylesheet>
```

Passing Parameters to XSLT Transformations

```
<?xml version="1.0" encoding="UTF-8"?>
<xsl:stylesheet version="1.0" xmlns:xsl="http://www.w3.org/1999/XSL/Transform">
  <xsl:param name="companyName" select="'ABC Inc.'"/>
  <xsl:template match="/">
    <html>
      <body>
        <h1>Welcome to <xsl:value-of select="$companyName"/></h1>
```

```
        </body>
      </html>
    </xsl:template>
</xsl:stylesheet>
```

Parsing XML using DOM (Document Object Model) in Java

```
<dependency>
    <groupId>org.w3c</groupId>
    <artifactId>dom</artifactId>
    <version>1.0.1</version>
</dependency>
```

Modifying XML using DOM in Java

```
<dependency>
    <groupId>org.w3c</groupId>
    <artifactId>dom</artifactId>
    <version>1.0.1</version>
</dependency>
```

Parsing XML using SAX (Simple API for XML) parser in Java

```
<dependency>
    <groupId>org.xml.sax</groupId>
    <artifactId>sax</artifactId>
    <version>2.0.1</version>
</dependency>
```

Validating XML using SAX parser in Java

```
<dependency>
    <groupId>org.xml.sax</groupId>
    <artifactId>sax</artifactId>
    <version>2.0.1</version>
```

```
</dependency>
```

Using JAXB (Java Architecture for XML Binding) for XML data binding

```
<dependency>
    <groupId>javax.xml.bind</groupId>
    <artifactId>jaxb-api</artifactId>
    <version>2.3.1</version>
</dependency>
```

Marshalling and Unmarshalling XML using JAXB in Java

```
<dependency>
    <groupId>javax.xml.bind</groupId>
    <artifactId>jaxb-api</artifactId>
    <version>2.3.1</version>
</dependency>
```

Parsing XML using JAXP (Java API for XML Processing) in Java

```
<dependency>
    <groupId>javax.xml</groupId>
    <artifactId>javax.xml-api</artifactId>
    <version>1.0.1</version>
</dependency>
```

Generating XML using JAXP in Java

```
<dependency>
    <groupId>javax.xml</groupId>
    <artifactId>jaxp-api</artifactId>
    <version>1.4.5</version>
</dependency>
```

Using XML Serialization and Deserialization in Java

```
<dependency>
    <groupId>javax.xml.bind</groupId>
    <artifactId>jaxb-api</artifactId>
    <version>2.3.1</version>
</dependency>
```

Converting XML to JSON using Jackson library in Java

```
<dependency>
    <groupId>com.fasterxml.jackson.dataformat</groupId>
    <artifactId>jackson-dataformat-xml</artifactId>
    <version>2.12.5</version>
</dependency>
```

Converting JSON to XML using Jackson library in Java

```
<dependency>
    <groupId>com.fasterxml.jackson.dataformat</groupId>
    <artifactId>jackson-dataformat-xml</artifactId>
    <version>2.12.5</version>
</dependency>
```

Parsing XML with ElementTree in Python

```
<dependency>
    <groupId>xml.etree.ElementTree</groupId>
    <artifactId>ElementTree</artifactId>
    <version>1.3.0</version>
</dependency>
```

Modifying XML with ElementTree in Python

```
<dependency>
    <groupId>xml.etree.ElementTree</groupId>
```

```
<artifactId>ElementTree</artifactId>
<version>1.3.0</version>
</dependency>
```

Validating XML with lxml in Python

```
<dependency>
<groupId>lxml</groupId>
<artifactId>lxml</artifactId>
<version>4.7.0</version>
</dependency>
```

Performing XPath queries in Python using lxml

```
<dependency>
<groupId>lxml</groupId>
<artifactId>lxml</artifactId>
<version>4.7.0</version>
</dependency>
```

Parse and Generate XML using JavaScript (DOM)

```html
<!DOCTYPE html>
<html lang="en">
<head>
  <meta charset="UTF-8">
  <meta name="viewport" content="width=device-width, initial-scale=1.0">
  <title>Parse and Generate XML using JavaScript (DOM)</title>
</head>
<body>
  <script>
    // Parsing XML using JavaScript DOM
    let xmlString = '<bookstore><book><title>Harry Potter</title><author>J.K. Rowling</author></book></bookstore>';
```

```javascript
      let parser = new DOMParser();
      let xmlDoc = parser.parseFromString(xmlString, "text/xml");

      // Generating XML using JavaScript DOM
      let newBook = xmlDoc.createElement("book");
      let newTitle = xmlDoc.createElement("title");
      newTitle.textContent = "The Hobbit";
      let newAuthor = xmlDoc.createElement("author");
      newAuthor.textContent = "J.R.R. Tolkien";
      newBook.appendChild(newTitle);
      newBook.appendChild(newAuthor);
      xmlDoc.getElementsByTagName("bookstore")[0].appendChild(newBook);

      console.log(xmlDoc.documentElement.outerHTML);
    </script>
  </body>
</html>
```

Parse XML using JavaScript (SAX)

```html
<script src="https://cdnjs.cloudflare.com/ajax/libs/sax/1.2.4/sax.min.js"></script>
<script>
   var saxParser = sax.parser(true);
   saxParser.onerror = function (e) {
     console.error('Error parsing XML:', e);
   };

   saxParser.ontext = function (t) {
     console.log('Text:', t);
   };

   saxParser.write('<book><title>Harry Potter</title></book>').close();
```

```
</script>
```

Read and Write XML Files in C#

```xml
<Project Sdk="Microsoft.NET.Sdk">
  <PropertyGroup>
    <OutputType>Exe</OutputType>
    <TargetFramework>net6.0</TargetFramework>
  </PropertyGroup>


  <ItemGroup>
    <PackageReference Include="System.Xml.XmlDocument" Version="5.0.0" />
  </ItemGroup>


</Project>
```

Validate XML in C#

```xml
<Project Sdk="Microsoft.NET.Sdk">
  <PropertyGroup>
    <OutputType>Exe</OutputType>
    <TargetFramework>net6.0</TargetFramework>
  </PropertyGroup>


  <ItemGroup>
    <PackageReference Include="System.Xml.Schema" Version="5.0.0" />
  </ItemGroup>
</Project>
```

Use LINQ to XML in C#

```xml
<Project Sdk="Microsoft.NET.Sdk">
  <PropertyGroup>
    <OutputType>Exe</OutputType>
```

```
    <TargetFramework>net6.0</TargetFramework>
  </PropertyGroup>


  <ItemGroup>
    <PackageReference Include="System.Xml.Linq" Version="5.0.0" />
  </ItemGroup>


</Project>
```


Parse XML in Perl using XML::LibXML module

```
<dependency>
    <groupId>cpan</groupId>
    <artifactId>XML-LibXML</artifactId>
    <version>2.0201</version>
</dependency>
```


Use XML::Simple module for XML parsing in Perl

```
<dependency>
    <groupId>cpan</groupId>
    <artifactId>XML-Simple</artifactId>
    <version>2.25</version>
</dependency>
```


Parse and Manipulate XML in PHP

```
<dependency>
    <groupId>php</groupId>
    <artifactId>php-xml</artifactId>
    <version>7.4</version>
</dependency>
```

Generate XML from Database Queries in PHP

```php
<?php
// Connect to database
$pdo = new PDO('mysql:host=localhost;dbname=mydatabase', 'username', 'password');
// Prepare and execute query
$stmt = $pdo->prepare('SELECT * FROM books');
$stmt->execute();
// Generate XML output
header('Content-Type: application/xml');
echo '<?xml version="1.0" encoding="UTF-8"?>';
echo '<books>';

while ($row = $stmt->fetch(PDO::FETCH_ASSOC)) {
    echo '<book>';
    echo '<title>' . htmlspecialchars($row['title']) . '</title>';
    echo '<author>' . htmlspecialchars($row['author']) . '</author>';
    echo '<genre>' . htmlspecialchars($row['genre']) . '</genre>';
    echo '<price>' . htmlspecialchars($row['price']) . '</price>';
    echo '</book>';
}
echo '</books>';
?>
```

Implement XML-RPC Client and Server in Python

```python
# XML-RPC Server
from xmlrpc.server import SimpleXMLRPCServer
def add(x, y):
    return x + y
server = SimpleXMLRPCServer(('localhost', 8000))
server.register_function(add, 'add')
```

```
server.serve_forever()


# XML-RPC Client
import xmlrpc.client
proxy = xmlrpc.client.ServerProxy('http://localhost:8000')
result = proxy.add(3, 5)
print("Result:", result)
```

Implement SOAP (Simple Object Access Protocol) Web Services

```
# SOAP Server
from spyne import Application, rpc, ServiceBase, Iterable, Integer, Unicode
class HelloWorldService(ServiceBase):
    @rpc(Unicode, Integer, _returns=Iterable(Unicode))
    def say_hello(ctx, name, times):
        for i in range(times):
            yield 'Hello, %s' % name
application = Application([HelloWorldService], tns='spyne.examples.hello',
in_protocol=None, out_protocol=None)


# SOAP Client
from suds.client import Client
client = Client('http://localhost:8000/?wsdl')
result = client.service.say_hello('John', 3)
print(result)
```

Create RSS Feeds in XML Format

```
<?xml version="1.0" encoding="UTF-8"?>
<rss version="2.0">
  <channel>
    <title>My Blog</title>
    <link>http://www.example.com/blog</link>
```

```
    <description>This is my blog</description>
    <item>
      <title>First Post</title>
      <link>http://www.example.com/blog/first-post</link>
      <description>Welcome to my first post</description>
    </item>
    <item>
      <title>Second Post</title>
      <link>http://www.example.com/blog/second-post</link>
      <description>Read about the second post</description>
    </item>
  </channel>
</rss>
```

Parse Atom Feeds using XML

```
import feedparser
feed = feedparser.parse('http://example.com/feed.atom')
for entry in feed.entries:
    print(entry.title)
    print(entry.link)
    print(entry.summary)
    print()
```

Parse SVG (Scalable Vector Graphics) with XML

```
<?xml version="1.0" encoding="UTF-8"?>
<svg width="100" height="100">
  <circle cx="50" cy="50" r="40" stroke="black" stroke-width="3" fill="red" />
</svg>
```

Transform XML using XSL-FO (XSL Formatting Objects)

```xml
<?xml version="1.0" encoding="UTF-8"?>
<xsl:stylesheet version="1.0" xmlns:xsl="http://www.w3.org/1999/XSL/Transform">
  <xsl:template match="/">
    <fo:root xmlns:fo="http://www.w3.org/1999/XSL/Format">
      <fo:layout-master-set>
        <fo:simple-page-master master-name="page" page-height="11in" page-width="8.5in">
          <fo:region-body margin="1in"/>
        </fo:simple-page-master>
      </fo:layout-master-set>
      <fo:page-sequence master-reference="page">
        <fo:flow flow-name="xsl-region-body">
          <fo:block font-size="12pt" font-family="Arial">
            <xsl:apply-templates/>
          </fo:block>
        </fo:flow>
      </fo:page-sequence>
    </fo:root>
  </xsl:template>
</xsl:stylesheet>
```

Use XML for Configuration Files in Software Development

```xml
<?xml version="1.0" encoding="UTF-8"?>
<config>
  <database>
    <host>localhost</host>
    <port>3306</port>
    <username>myuser</username>
    <password>mypassword</password>
  </database>
```

```
<log>
  <level>debug</level>
  <file>/var/log/myapp.log</file>
</log>
</config>
```

Parse XML Responses from APIs in Android Applications

```
// Example parsing XML using XmlPullParser in Android
XmlPullParser parser = Xml.newPullParser();
parser.setFeature(XmlPullParser.FEATURE_PROCESS_NAMESPACES, false);
parser.setInput(new StringReader(xmlString));

int eventType = parser.getEventType();
while (eventType != XmlPullParser.END_DOCUMENT) {
   if (eventType == XmlPullParser.START_TAG) {
      String tagName = parser.getName();
      // Handle parsing logic based on tag name
   }
   eventType = parser.next();
}
```

Use XML Layout Files in Android Development

```
<!-- Example of an XML layout file in Android development -->
<?xml version="1.0" encoding="utf-8"?>
<LinearLayout xmlns:android="http://schemas.android.com/apk/res/android"
   android:layout_width="match_parent"
   android:layout_height="match_parent"
   android:orientation="vertical" >

   <TextView
      android:id="@+id/textView"
```

```
    android:layout_width="wrap_content"

    android:layout_height="wrap_content"

    android:text="Hello, Android!"

    android:textSize="24sp"

    android:layout_gravity="center_horizontal" />


  <Button

    android:id="@+id/button"

    android:layout_width="wrap_content"

    android:layout_height="wrap_content"

    android:text="Click Me"

    android:layout_gravity="center_horizontal" />


</LinearLayout>
```

Parse XML Configuration Files in Spring Framework

```
<!-- Example of parsing XML configuration files in Spring Framework -->
<beans xmlns="http://www.springframework.org/schema/beans"
    xmlns:xsi="http://www.w3.org/2001/XMLSchema-instance"
    xsi:schemaLocation="http://www.springframework.org/schema/beans
            http://www.springframework.org/schema/beans/spring-beans.xsd">

  <bean id="myBean" class="com.example.MyBean">
    <property name="name" value="John" />
    <property name="age" value="30" />
  </bean>

</beans>
```

Use XML for Messaging with JMS (Java Messaging Service)

```xml
<!-- Example of using XML for messaging with JMS (Java Messaging Service) -->
<message>
  <header>
    <sender>sender@example.com</sender>
    <recipient>recipient@example.com</recipient>
    <subject>Hello!</subject>
  </header>
  <body>
    <content>Hello, this is a message.</content>
  </body>
</message>
```

Implement XML Data Binding in .NET

```xml
<!-- Example of implementing XML data binding in .NET -->
<xs:schema xmlns:xs="http://www.w3.org/2001/XMLSchema">
  <xs:element name="person">
    <xs:complexType>
      <xs:sequence>
        <xs:element name="name" type="xs:string"/>
        <xs:element name="age" type="xs:int"/>
      </xs:sequence>
    </xs:complexType>
  </xs:element>
</xs:schema>
```

Serialize and Deserialize XML in .NET

```xml
<!-- Example of serializing and deserializing XML in .NET -->
<person>
  <name>John Doe</name>
  <age>30</age>
```

```
</person>
```

Use XPath Queries in .NET

```
<!-- Example of using XPath queries in .NET -->
// C# code to select nodes using XPath
XmlNodeList nodeList = xmlDoc.SelectNodes("/books/book[price > 20]");
```

Use XQuery to Query XML Data

```
<!-- Example of using XQuery to query XML data -->
for $book in doc("books.xml")//book
where $book/price > 20
return $book/title
```

Implement XQuery Expressions and Functions

```
<!-- Example of implementing XQuery expressions and functions -->
let $total := sum(for $item in doc("orders.xml")//item return $item/price *
$item/quantity)
return $total
```

Use XML for Creating Multimedia Presentations (SMIL)

```
<!-- Example of using XML for creating multimedia presentations (SMIL) -->
<smil>
  <head>
    <layout>
      <root-layout width="800px" height="600px" />
      <region id="main" width="80%" height="80%" left="10%" top="10%" />
    </layout>
  </head>
  <body>
    <seq>
      <video src="video1.mp4" region="main" />
```

```
      <audio src="audio1.mp3" region="main" />

    </seq>

  </body>

</smil>
```

Implement XML for Representing Business Processes (BPEL)

```
<!-- Example of using XML for representing business processes (BPEL) -->

<process name="OrderProcess" xmlns="http://docs.oasis-

open.org/wsbpel/2.0/process/executable">

  <sequence>

    <receive name="receiveOrder" partnerLink="client" portType="tns:orderPT"

operation="submitOrder" />

    <invoke name="processOrder" partnerLink="inventory"

portType="tns:inventoryPT" operation="checkInventory" />

    <reply name="replyOrder" partnerLink="client"

operation="submitOrderResponse" />

  </sequence>

</process>
```

Use XML for Representing Vector Graphics (SVG)

```
<!-- Example of using XML for representing vector graphics (SVG) -->

<svg width="100" height="100">

  <circle cx="50" cy="50" r="40" stroke="black" stroke-width="2" fill="red" />

</svg>
```

Implement XML for Representing Mathematical Formulas (MathML)

```
<!-- Example of using XML for representing mathematical formulas (MathML) -->

<math xmlns="http://www.w3.org/1998/Math/MathML">

  <mrow>

    <msup>

      <mi>x</mi>
```

```
        <mn>2</mn>
      </msup>
      <mo>+</mo>
      <mi>y</mi>
      <mo>=</mo>
      <mn>10</mn>
    </mrow>
</math>
```

Use XML for Representing Chemical Structures (CML)

```
<!-- Example of using XML for representing chemical structures (CML) -->
<cml xmlns="http://www.xml-cml.org/schema">
    <molecule title="Benzene">
      <atomArray>
        <atom id="a1" elementType="C" x3="-1.394" y3="-0.202" z3="0.000" />
        <atom id="a2" elementType="C" x3="-0.264" y3="1.198" z3="0.000" />
        <!-- Additional atoms and bonds -->
      </atomArray>
    </molecule>
</cml>
```

Implement XML for Representing User Interface Layouts (XUL)

```
<!-- Example of using XML for representing user interface layouts (XUL) -->
<?xml version="1.0"?>
<?xml-stylesheet href="chrome://global/skin/" type="text/css"?>

<window xmlns="http://www.mozilla.org/keymaster/gatekeeper/there.is.only.xul"
    title="Hello World"
    width="200"
    height="100">
```

```
<vbox flex="1">
   <label value="Hello, World!" />
   <button label="Click Me" oncommand="alert('Button clicked!');" />
</vbox>
</window>
```

Use XML for Representing Syndicated Content (RSS, Atom)

```
<!-- Example of using XML for representing syndicated content (RSS, Atom) -->
<rss version="2.0">
   <channel>
      <title>My Blog</title>
      <link>http://www.example.com/blog</link>
      <description>This is my blog</description>
      <item>
         <title>First Post</title>
         <link>http://www.example.com/blog/first-post</link>
         <description>Welcome to my first post</description>
      </item>
      <item>
         <title>Second Post</title>
         <link>http://www.example.com/blog/second-post</link>
         <description>Read about the second post</description>
      </item>
   </channel>
</rss>
```

Implement XML for Representing User Profiles (XUP)

```
<!-- Example of using XML for representing user profiles (XUP) -->
<userProfile xmlns="http://www.example.com/profile">
   <username>john_doe</username>
   <firstName>John</firstName>
```

```
    <lastName>Doe</lastName>

    <email>john@example.com</email>

    <birthdate>1990-05-15</birthdate>

    <location>

      <city>New York</city>

      <state>NY</state>

      <country>USA</country>

    </location>

</userProfile>
```

Use XML for Representing Geospatial Data (GML)

```
<!-- Example of using XML for representing geospatial data (GML) -->

<gml:Point xmlns:gml="http://www.opengis.net/gml">

  <gml:pos>51.5007 -0.1246</gml:pos>

</gml:Point>
```

Implement XML for Representing Calendar Data (iCalendar)

```
<!-- Example of using XML for representing calendar data (iCalendar) -->

<icalendar xmlns="http://www.example.com/calendar">

  <event>

    <summary>Team Meeting</summary>

    <start>2024-04-30T10:00:00</start>

    <end>2024-04-30T11:00:00</end>

    <location>Conference Room A</location>

  </event>

  <event>

    <summary>Project Deadline</summary>

    <start>2024-05-15T09:00:00</start>

    <end>2024-05-15T17:00:00</end>

    <location>Office</location>

  </event>
```

```
</icalendar>
```

Use XML for Representing 3D Graphics (X3D)

```
<!-- Example of using XML for representing 3D graphics (X3D) -->
<X3D xmlns="http://www.web3d.org/specifications/x3d-3.3">
  <Scene>
    <Shape>
      <Appearance>
        <Material diffuseColor="1 0 0" />
      </Appearance>
      <Box size="2 2 2" />
    </Shape>
  </Scene>
</X3D>
```

Implement XML for Representing Genealogical Data (GEDCOM)

```
<!-- Example of using XML for representing genealogical data (GEDCOM) -->
<gedcom>
  <individual>
    <name>John Doe</name>
    <birth>
      <date>1990-05-15</date>
      <place>New York, USA</place>
    </birth>
    <parents>
      <father>Michael Doe</father>
      <mother>Jane Doe</mother>
    </parents>
  </individual>
</gedcom>
```

Use XML for Representing Electronic Books (ePub)

```xml
<!-- Example of using XML for representing electronic books (ePub) -->
<package xmlns="http://www.idpf.org/2007/opf" unique-identifier="bookid">
  <metadata>
    <dc:title>My Book</dc:title>
    <dc:creator>John Doe</dc:creator>
    <dc:date>2024-04-30</dc:date>
  </metadata>
  <manifest>
    <item id="cover" href="cover.jpg" media-type="image/jpeg" />
    <item id="chapter1" href="chapter1.html" media-type="text/html" />
    <!-- Additional book content -->
  </manifest>
  <spine>
    <itemref idref="cover" />
    <itemref idref="chapter1" />
    <!-- Additional chapters -->
  </spine>
</package>
```

Implement XML for Representing Bibliographic References (MODS)

```xml
<!-- Example of using XML for representing bibliographic references (MODS) -->
<mods xmlns="http://www.loc.gov/mods/v3">
  <titleInfo>
    <title>My Book</title>
  </titleInfo>
  <name type="personal">
    <namePart>Doe, John</namePart>
  </name>
  <originInfo>
    <dateIssued>2024</dateIssued>
```

```
    </originInfo>
  </mods>
```

Use XML for Representing Chemical Data (CDXML)

```
<!-- Example of using XML for representing chemical data (CDXML) -->
<cdxml xmlns="http://www.cambridgesoft.com/xml/cdxml">
  <page>
    <object type="shape" display="full">
      <graphic type="shape" subtype="circle" x="100" y="100" width="50"
height="50" />
    </object>
  </page>
</cdxml>
```

Implement XML for Representing Music Scores (MusicXML)

```
<!-- Example of using XML for representing music scores (MusicXML) -->
<score-partwise version="3.1">
  <part-list>
    <score-part id="P1">
      <part-name>Music Staff</part-name>
    </score-part>
  </part-list>
  <part id="P1">
    <measure number="1">
      <note>
        <pitch>
          <step>C</step>
          <octave>4</octave>
        </pitch>
        <duration>4</duration>
        <type>quarter</type>
```

```
      </note>

      <!-- Additional notes and musical elements -->

    </measure>

  </part>

</score-partwise>
```

Use XML for Representing Statistical Data (SDMX)

```
<!-- Example of using XML for representing statistical data (SDMX) -->

<Structure xmlns="http://www.sdmx.org/resources/sdmxml/schemas/v2_1/message">

  <CodeLists>

    <CodeList id="CL_COUNTRY">

      <Code value="US">United States</Code>

      <Code value="FR">France</Code>

      <!-- Additional country codes -->

    </CodeList>

  </CodeLists>

  <Data>

    <Series>

      <SeriesKey>

        <Value concept="COUNTRY" value="US" />

        <Value concept="INDICATOR" value="GDP" />

      </SeriesKey>

      <Obs>

        <ObsValue value="21500" />

      </Obs>

      <!-- Additional observations -->

    </Series>

  </Data>

</Structure>
```

Implement XML for Representing Electronic Health Records (CDA)

```xml
<!-- Example of using XML for representing electronic health records (CDA) -->
<ClinicalDocument xmlns="urn:hl7-org:v3"
xmlns:xsi="http://www.w3.org/2001/XMLSchema-instance">
   <title>Medical Record</title>
   <patient>
      <name>John Doe</name>
      <dob>1990-05-15</dob>
      <!-- Additional patient information -->
   </patient>
   <encounter>
      <date>2024-04-30</date>
      <provider>Dr. Smith</provider>
      <!-- Additional encounter details -->
   </encounter>
   <!-- Additional health record data -->
</ClinicalDocument>
```

Use XML for Representing Legal Documents (LegalXML)

```xml
<!-- Example of using XML for representing legal documents (LegalXML) -->
<LegalDocument xmlns="http://www.legalxml.org/schema/legalxml-courtfiling/3.0">
   <Case>
      <CaseNumber>12345</CaseNumber>
      <Court>
         <CourtName>Supreme Court</CourtName>
         <CourtLocation>Washington, DC</CourtLocation>
      </Court>
      <!-- Additional case details -->
   </Case>
   <Parties>
      <Plaintiff>John Doe</Plaintiff>
```

```xml
      <Defendant>Jane Smith</Defendant>
      <!-- Additional parties involved -->
   </Parties>
   <!-- Additional legal document content -->
</LegalDocument>
```

Implement XML for Representing Educational Content (SCORM)

```xml
<!-- Example of using XML for representing educational content (SCORM) -->
<manifest xmlns="http://www.imsproject.org/xsd/imscp_rootv1p1p2"
xmlns:adlcp="http://www.adlnet.org/xsd/adlcp_rootv1p2"
xmlns:xsi="http://www.w3.org/2001/XMLSchema-instance">
   <metadata>
     <schema>ADL SCORM</schema>
     <!-- Additional metadata -->
   </metadata>
   <organizations>
     <organization identifier="org1">
        <title>My Course</title>
        <!-- Additional organization details -->
     </organization>
   </organizations>
   <!-- Additional content structure -->
</manifest>
```

Use XML for Representing Financial Transactions (OFX)

```xml
<!-- Example of using XML for representing financial transactions (OFX) -->
<OFX xmlns="http://www.ofx.net/schemas/2003/06">
   <SIGNONMSGSRSV1>
     <SONRS>
       <STATUS>
          <CODE>0</CODE>
```

```xml
        <SEVERITY>INFO</SEVERITY>
      </STATUS>
      <!-- Additional sign-on response details -->
    </SONRS>
  </SIGNONMSGSRSV1>
  <BANKMSGSRSV1>
    <STMTTRNRS>
      <TRNUID>12345</TRNUID>
      <!-- Additional statement transaction response -->
    </STMTTRNRS>
  </BANKMSGSRSV1>
</OFX>
```

Implement XML for Representing Project Management Data (MPX)

```xml
<!-- Example of using XML for representing project management data (MPX) -->
<Project xmlns="http://schemas.microsoft.com/project">
  <Tasks>
    <Task>
      <Name>Task 1</Name>
      <StartDate>2024-04-30</StartDate>
      <FinishDate>2024-05-05</FinishDate>
      <!-- Additional task details -->
    </Task>
  </Tasks>
  <!-- Additional project data -->
</Project>
```

Use XML for Representing Structured Documents (DocBook)

```xml
<!-- Example of using XML for representing structured documents (DocBook) -->
<article xmlns="http://docbook.org/ns/docbook">
  <title>Sample Document</title>
```

```xml
  <section>
    <title>Introduction</title>
    <para>This is a sample document.</para>
  </section>
  <!-- Additional document sections -->
</article>
```

Implement XML for Representing Syndicated Web Content (RDF)

```xml
<!-- Example of using XML for representing syndicated web content (RDF) -->
<rdf:RDF xmlns:rdf="http://www.w3.org/1999/02/22-rdf-syntax-ns#"
xmlns:dc="http://purl.org/dc/elements/1.1/">
  <rdf:Description rdf:about="http://www.example.com/article1">
    <dc:title>Article 1</dc:title>
    <dc:creator>John Doe</dc:creator>
    <dc:date>2024-04-30</dc:date>
  </rdf:Description>
  <!-- Additional RDF descriptions -->
</rdf:RDF>
```

Use XML for Representing Remote Procedure Calls (XML-RPC)

```xml
<!-- Example of using XML for representing remote procedure calls (XML-RPC) -->
<methodCall>
  <methodName>examples.getStateName</methodName>
  <params>
    <param>
      <value><int>41</int></value>
    </param>
  </params>
</methodCall>
```

Implement XML for Representing Mathematical Markup (MathML)

```xml
<!-- Example of using XML for representing mathematical markup (MathML) -->
<math xmlns="http://www.w3.org/1998/Math/MathML">
   <mrow>
     <msup>
       <mi>x</mi>
       <mn>2</mn>
     </msup>
     <mo>+</mo>
     <mi>y</mi>
     <mo>=</mo>
     <mn>10</mn>
   </mrow>
</math>
```

Use XML for Representing Chemical Data (CML)

```xml
<!-- Example of using XML for representing chemical data (CML) -->
<cml xmlns="http://www.xml-cml.org/schema">
   <molecule title="Benzene">
     <atomArray>
       <atom id="a1" elementType="C" x3="-1.394" y3="-0.202" z3="0.000" />
       <atom id="a2" elementType="C" x3="-0.264" y3="1.198" z3="0.000" />
       <!-- Additional atoms and bonds -->
     </atomArray>
   </molecule>
</cml>
```

Implement XML for Representing GIS Data (GML)

```xml
<!-- Example of using XML for representing GIS data (GML) -->
<gml:Point xmlns:gml="http://www.opengis.net/gml">
   <gml:pos>51.5007 -0.1246</gml:pos>
```

```
</gml:Point>
```

Use XML for Representing E-commerce Transactions (UBL)

```
<!-- Example of using XML for representing e-commerce transactions (UBL) -->
<Invoice xmlns="urn:oasis:names:specification:ubl:schema:xsd:Invoice-2"

xmlns:cac="urn:oasis:names:specification:ubl:schema:xsd:CommonAggregateCompone
nts-2">
    <ID>123456</ID>
    <IssueDate>2024-04-30</IssueDate>
    <AccountingSupplierParty>
      <Party>
        <PartyName>XYZ Corporation</PartyName>
        <!-- Additional supplier details -->
      </Party>
    </AccountingSupplierParty>
    <!-- Additional invoice data -->
</Invoice>
```

Implement XML for Representing Multimedia Presentations (SMIL)

```
<!-- Example of using XML for representing multimedia presentations (SMIL) -->
<smil xmlns="http://www.w3.org/2001/SMIL20/Language">
    <body>
      <par>
        <img src="image1.jpg" />
        <text src="text1.txt" />
        <!-- Additional multimedia elements -->
      </par>
    </body>
</smil>
```

Use XML for Representing User Interfaces (XUL)

```xml
<!-- Example of using XML for representing user interfaces (XUL) -->
<?xml version="1.0"?>
<window xmlns="http://www.mozilla.org/keymaster/gatekeeper/there.is.only.xul"
    title="My Application" width="400" height="300">
  <vbox>
    <label value="Welcome to My Application!" />
    <button label="Click Me" oncommand="alert('Button clicked!');" />
  </vbox>
</window>
```

Implement XML for Representing Digital Books (EPUB)

```xml
<!-- Example of using XML for representing digital books (EPUB) -->
<package xmlns="http://www.idpf.org/2007/opf" unique-identifier="bookid">
  <metadata>
    <dc:title>My Book</dc:title>
    <dc:creator>John Doe</dc:creator>
    <dc:date>2024-04-30</dc:date>
  </metadata>
  <manifest>
    <item id="cover" href="cover.jpg" media-type="image/jpeg" />
    <item id="chapter1" href="chapter1.html" media-type="text/html" />
    <!-- Additional book content -->
  </manifest>
  <spine>
    <itemref idref="cover" />
    <itemref idref="chapter1" />
    <!-- Additional chapters -->
  </spine>
</package>
```

Use XML for Representing Bibliographic Information (MODS)

```xml
<!-- Example of using XML for representing bibliographic information (MODS) -->
<mods xmlns="http://www.loc.gov/mods/v3">
  <titleInfo>
    <title>My Book</title>
  </titleInfo>
  <name type="personal">
    <namePart>Doe, John</namePart>
  </name>
  <originInfo>
    <dateIssued>2024</dateIssued>
  </originInfo>
</mods>
```

Implement XML for Representing News Syndication (RSS/ATOM)

```xml
<!-- Example of using XML for representing news syndication (RSS/ATOM) -->
<rss version="2.0">
  <channel>
    <title>My News Feed</title>
    <link>http://www.example.com/news</link>
    <description>Latest news updates</description>
    <item>
      <title>Breaking News</title>
      <link>http://www.example.com/news/breaking</link>
      <description>Read about the breaking news</description>
    </item>
    <!-- Additional news items -->
  </channel>
</rss>
```

Use XML for Representing Genealogy Data (GEDCOM)

```xml
<!-- Example of using XML for representing genealogy data (GEDCOM) -->
<gedcom>
  <individual>
    <name>John Doe</name>
    <birth>
      <date>1990-05-15</date>
      <place>New York, USA</place>
    </birth>
    <parents>
      <father>Michael Doe</father>
      <mother>Jane Doe</mother>
    </parents>
  </individual>
</gedcom>
```

Implement XML for Representing Multimedia Content (SVG)

```xml
<!-- Example of using XML for representing multimedia content (SVG) -->
<svg xmlns="http://www.w3.org/2000/svg" width="400" height="200">
  <circle cx="100" cy="100" r="50" fill="red" />
  <rect x="200" y="50" width="150" height="100" fill="blue" />
  <!-- Additional SVG elements -->
</svg>
```

Use XML for Representing Mathematical Formulas (MathML)

```xml
<!-- Example of using XML for representing mathematical formulas (MathML) -->
<math xmlns="http://www.w3.org/1998/Math/MathML">
  <mrow>
    <msup>
      <mi>x</mi>
      <mn>2</mn>
```

```
        </msup>
        <mo>+</mo>
        <mi>y</mi>
        <mo>=</mo>
        <mn>10</mn>
      </mrow>
</math>
```

Implement XML for Representing Geographic Data (GML)

```
<!-- Example of using XML for representing geographic data (GML) -->
<gml:Point xmlns:gml="http://www.opengis.net/gml">
   <gml:pos>51.5007 -0.1246</gml:pos>
</gml:Point>
```

Use XML for Representing Legal Documents (LegalXML)

```
<!-- Example of using XML for representing legal documents (LegalXML) -->
<LegalDocument xmlns="http://www.legalxml.org/schema/legalxml-courtfiling/3.0">
   <Case>
      <CaseNumber>12345</CaseNumber>
      <Court>
         <CourtName>Supreme Court</CourtName>
         <CourtLocation>Washington, DC</CourtLocation>
      </Court>
      <!-- Additional case details -->
   </Case>
   <Parties>
      <Plaintiff>John Doe</Plaintiff>
      <Defendant>Jane Smith</Defendant>
      <!-- Additional parties involved -->
   </Parties>
   <!-- Additional legal document content -->
```

```
</LegalDocument>
```

Implement XML for Representing Educational Content (SCORM)

```
<!-- Example of using XML for representing educational content (SCORM) -->
<manifest xmlns="http://www.imsproject.org/xsd/imscp_rootv1p1p2"
xmlns:adlcp="http://www.adlnet.org/xsd/adlcp_rootv1p2"
xmlns:xsi="http://www.w3.org/2001/XMLSchema-instance">
  <metadata>
    <schema>ADL SCORM</schema>
    <!-- Additional metadata -->
  </metadata>
  <organizations>
    <organization identifier="org1">
      <title>My Course</title>
      <!-- Additional organization details -->
    </organization>
  </organizations>
  <!-- Additional content structure -->
</manifest>
```

Use XML for Representing Financial Data (XBRL)

```
<!-- Example of using XML for representing financial data (XBRL) -->
<xbrl xmlns="http://www.xbrl.org/2003/instance">
  <context>
    <entity>
      <identifier scheme="http://www.sec.gov/CIK">0001018724</identifier>
      &lt;segment&gt;
        <explicitMember dimension="us-gaap:BusinessSegmentAxis">us-gaap:Domestic</explicitMember>
      &lt;/segment&gt;
    </entity>
```

```xml
      <period>
        <startDate>2024-01-01</startDate>
        <endDate>2024-12-31</endDate>
      </period>
    </context>
    <fact>
      <value>1000000</value>
      <concept>us-gaap:Revenues</concept>
      <unit>iso4217:USD</unit>
      <contextRef>CONTEXT1</contextRef>
    </fact>
    <!-- Additional financial data -->
</xbrl>
```

Implement XML for Representing Project Data (MPX)

```xml
<!-- Example of using XML for representing project data (MPX) -->
<project xmlns="http://schemas.microsoft.com/project">
    <tasks>
      <task>
        <name>Task 1</name>
        <start>2024-04-30</start>
        <finish>2024-05-05</finish>
        <!-- Additional task details -->
      </task>
    </tasks>
    <!-- Additional project data -->
</project>
```

Use XML for Representing Web Services (WSDL)

```xml
<!-- Example of using XML for representing web services (WSDL) -->
<definitions xmlns="http://schemas.xmlsoap.org/wsdl/"
```

```
      xmlns:soap="http://schemas.xmlsoap.org/wsdl/soap/"
      xmlns:xsd="http://www.w3.org/2001/XMLSchema"
      name="MyWebService"
      targetNamespace="http://example.com/wsdl">
  <types>
    <xsd:schema>
      <!-- Define data types -->
    </xsd:schema>
  </types>
  <message name="RequestMessage">
    <!-- Define request message structure -->
  </message>
  <message name="ResponseMessage">
    <!-- Define response message structure -->
  </message>
  <portType name="MyWebServicePortType">
    <operation name="MyOperation">
      <input message="tns:RequestMessage"/>
      <output message="tns:ResponseMessage"/>
    </operation>
  </portType>
  <binding name="MyWebServiceBinding" type="tns:MyWebServicePortType">
    <soap:binding style="rpc" transport="http://schemas.xmlsoap.org/soap/http"/>
    <operation name="MyOperation">
      <soap:operation soapAction="http://example.com/MyOperation"/>
      <input>
        <soap:body use="encoded" namespace="http://example.com/wsdl"/>
      </input>
      <output>
        <soap:body use="encoded" namespace="http://example.com/wsdl"/>
      </output>
```

```xml
    </operation>
  </binding>
  <service name="MyWebService">
    <port name="MyWebServicePort" binding="tns:MyWebServiceBinding">
      <soap:address location="http://example.com/MyWebService"/>
    </port>
  </service>
</definitions>
```

Implement XML for Representing Business Processes (BPEL)

```xml
<!-- Example of using XML for representing business processes (BPEL) -->
<process xmlns="http://docs.oasis-open.org/wsbpel/2.0/process/executable"
      xmlns:tns="http://example.com/bpel"
      targetNamespace="http://example.com/bpel">
  <sequence>
    <receive partnerLink="client" operation="Operation1" variable="input"/>
    <invoke partnerLink="service1" operation="Operation2" inputVariable="input"
outputVariable="output"/>
    <reply partnerLink="client" operation="Operation1" variable="output"/>
  </sequence>
</process>
```

Use XML for Representing Healthcare Data (CDA)

```xml
<!-- Example of using XML for representing healthcare data (CDA) -->
<ClinicalDocument xmlns="urn:hl7-org:v3">
  <title>Medical Record</title>
  <patient>
    <name>John Doe</name>
    <dob>1990-05-15</dob>
    <!-- Additional patient information -->
  </patient>
```

```xml
  <encounter>
    <date>2024-04-30</date>
    <provider>Dr. Smith</provider>
    <!-- Additional encounter details -->
  </encounter>
  <!-- Additional healthcare data -->
</ClinicalDocument>
```

Implement XML for Representing Office Documents (OpenXML)

```xml
<!-- Example of using XML for representing office documents (OpenXML) -->
<officeDocument
xmlns="http://schemas.openxmlformats.org/officeDocument/2006/relationships">
  <document>
    <paragraph>This is an example of an office document.</paragraph>
    <!-- Additional document content -->
  </document>
</officeDocument>
```

Use XML for Representing Electronic Books (EPUB)

```xml
<!-- Example of using XML for representing electronic books (EPUB) -->
<package xmlns="http://www.idpf.org/2007/opf" unique-identifier="bookid">
  <metadata>
    <dc:title>My Book</dc:title>
    <dc:creator>John Doe</dc:creator>
    <dc:date>2024-04-30</dc:date>
  </metadata>
  <manifest>
    <item id="cover" href="cover.jpg" media-type="image/jpeg" />
    <item id="chapter1" href="chapter1.html" media-type="text/html" />
    <!-- Additional book content -->
  </manifest>
```

```xml
  <spine>
    <itemref idref="cover" />
    <itemref idref="chapter1" />
    <!-- Additional chapters -->
  </spine>
</package>
```

Implement XML for Representing Bibliographic Data (MARC)

```xml
<!-- Example of using XML for representing bibliographic data (MARC) -->
<record xmlns="http://www.loc.gov/MARC21/slim">
  <leader>00000cam a2200000 a 4500</leader>
  <controlfield tag="001">123456</controlfield>
  <datafield tag="245" ind1="0" ind2="0">
    <subfield code="a">My Book</subfield>
  </datafield>
  <!-- Additional bibliographic data -->
</record>
```

Use XML for Representing Calendar Data (iCalendar)

```xml
<!-- Example of using XML for representing calendar data (iCalendar) -->
<icalendar xmlns="http://www.example.com/calendar">
  <event>
    <summary>Team Meeting</summary>
    <location>Conference Room A</location>
    <start>2024-05-01T09:00:00</start>
    <end>2024-05-01T10:00:00</end>
    <!-- Additional event details -->
  </event>
</icalendar>
```

Implement XML for Representing Metadata (Dublin Core)

```
<!-- Example of using XML for representing metadata (Dublin Core) -->
<metadata xmlns:dc="http://purl.org/dc/elements/1.1/">
  <dc:title>Document Title</dc:title>
  <dc:creator>John Doe</dc:creator>
  <dc:date>2024-04-30</dc:date>
  <!-- Additional Dublin Core metadata elements -->
</metadata>
```

Use XML for Representing Social Network Data (FOAF)

```
<!-- Example of using XML for representing social network data (FOAF) -->
<foaf:Person xmlns:foaf="http://xmlns.com/foaf/0.1/">
  <foaf:name>John Doe</foaf:name>
  <foaf:knows>
    <foaf:Person>
      <foaf:name>Jane Smith</foaf:name>
    </foaf:Person>
  </foaf:knows>
  <!-- Additional FOAF data -->
</foaf:Person>
```

Implement XML for Representing E-learning Content (SCORM)

```
<!-- Example of using XML for representing e-learning content (SCORM) -->
<manifest xmlns="http://www.imsproject.org/xsd/imscp_rootv1p1p2"
xmlns:adlcp="http://www.adlnet.org/xsd/adlcp_rootv1p2"
xmlns:xsi="http://www.w3.org/2001/XMLSchema-instance">
  <metadata>
    <schema>ADL SCORM</schema>
    <!-- Additional metadata -->
  </metadata>
  <organizations>
```

```xml
    <organization identifier="org1">

      <title>My Course</title>

      <!-- Additional organization details -->

    </organization>

  </organizations>

  <!-- Additional content structure -->

</manifest>
```

Use XML for Representing Financial Transactions (OFX)

```xml
<!-- Example of using XML for representing financial transactions (OFX) -->
<OFX xmlns="http://www.ofx.net/schemas/2003/06">

  <SIGNONMSGSRSV1>

    <SONRS>

      <STATUS>

        <CODE>0</CODE>

        <SEVERITY>INFO</SEVERITY>

      </STATUS>

      <!-- Additional sign-on response details -->

    </SONRS>

  </SIGNONMSGSRSV1>

  <BANKMSGSRSV1>

    <STMTTRNRS>

      <TRNUID>12345</TRNUID>

      <!-- Additional statement transaction response -->

    </STMTTRNRS>

  </BANKMSGSRSV1>

</OFX>
```

Implement XML for Representing Project Management Data (MPX)

```xml
<!-- Example of using XML for representing project management data (MPX) -->
<project xmlns="http://schemas.microsoft.com/project">
```

```
  <tasks>
    <task>
      <name>Task 1</name>
      <start>2024-04-30</start>
      <finish>2024-05-05</finish>
      <!-- Additional task details -->
    </task>
  </tasks>
  <!-- Additional project data -->
</project>
```

Use XML for Representing Structured Documents (DocBook)

```
<!-- Example of using XML for representing structured documents (DocBook) -->
<article xmlns="http://docbook.org/ns/docbook">
  <title>Sample Document</title>
  <section>
    <title>Introduction</title>
    <para>This is a sample document.</para>
  </section>
  <!-- Additional document sections -->
</article>
```

Implement XML for Representing Syndicated Web Content (RDF)

```
<!-- Example of using XML for representing syndicated web content (RDF) -->
<rdf:RDF xmlns:rdf="http://www.w3.org/1999/02/22-rdf-syntax-ns#"
xmlns:dc="http://purl.org/dc/elements/1.1/">
  <rdf:Description rdf:about="http://www.example.com/article1">
    <dc:title>Article 1</dc:title>
    <dc:creator>John Doe</dc:creator>
    <dc:date>2024-04-30</dc:date>
  </rdf:Description>
```

```
  <!-- Additional RDF descriptions -->
</rdf:RDF>
```

Use XML for Representing Remote Procedure Calls (XML-RPC)

```
<!-- Example of using XML for representing remote procedure calls (XML-RPC) -->
<methodCall>
  <methodName>examples.getStateName</methodName>
  <params>
    <param>
      <value><int>41</int></value>
    </param>
  </params>
</methodCall>
```

Implement XML for Representing Mathematical Markup (MathML)

```
<!-- Example of using XML for representing mathematical markup (MathML) -->
<math xmlns="http://www.w3.org/1998/Math/MathML">
  <mrow>
    <msup>
      <mi>x</mi>
      <mn>2</mn>
    </msup>
    <mo>+</mo>
    <mi>y</mi>
    <mo>=</mo>
    <mn>10</mn>
  </mrow>
</math>
```

Use XML for Representing Chemical Data (CML)

```
<!-- Example of using XML for representing chemical data (CML) -->
<cml xmlns="http://www.xml-cml.org/schema">
  <molecule title="Benzene">
    <atomArray>
      <atom id="a1" elementType="C" x3="-1.394" y3="-0.202" z3="0.000" />
      <atom id="a2" elementType="C" x3="-0.264" y3="1.198" z3="0.000" />
      <!-- Additional atoms and bonds -->
    </atomArray>
  </molecule>
</cml>
```

Implement XML for Representing GIS Data (GML)

```
<!-- Example of using XML for representing GIS data (GML) -->
<gml:Point xmlns:gml="http://www.opengis.net/gml">
  <gml:pos>51.5007 -0.1246</gml:pos>
</gml:Point>
```

Use XML for Representing E-commerce Transactions (UBL)

```
<!-- Example of using XML for representing e-commerce transactions (UBL) -->
<Invoice xmlns="urn:oasis:names:specification:ubl:schema:xsd:Invoice-2"

xmlns:cac="urn:oasis:names:specification:ubl:schema:xsd:CommonAggregateCompone
nts-2">
  <ID>123456</ID>
  <IssueDate>2024-04-30</IssueDate>
  <AccountingSupplierParty>
    <Party>
      <PartyName>XYZ Corporation</PartyName>
      <!-- Additional supplier details -->
    </Party>
```

```xml
  </AccountingSupplierParty>
  <!-- Additional invoice data -->
</Invoice>
```

Implement XML for Representing Multimedia Presentations (SMIL)

```xml
<!-- Example of using XML for representing multimedia presentations (SMIL) -->
<smil xmlns="http://www.w3.org/2001/SMIL20/Language">
  <body>
    <par>
      <img src="image1.jpg" />
      <text src="text1.txt" />
      <!-- Additional multimedia elements -->
    </par>
  </body>
</smil>
```

Use XML for Representing User Interfaces (XUL)

```xml
<!-- Example of using XML for representing user interfaces (XUL) -->
<?xml version="1.0"?>
<window xmlns="http://www.mozilla.org/keymaster/gatekeeper/there.is.only.xul"
    title="My Application" width="400" height="300">
  <vbox>
    <label value="Welcome to My Application!" />
    <button label="Click Me" oncommand="alert('Button clicked!');" />
  </vbox>
</window>
```

Implement XML for Representing Digital Books (EPUB)

```xml
<!-- Example of using XML for representing digital books (EPUB) -->
<package xmlns="http://www.idpf.org/2007/opf" unique-identifier="bookid">
  <metadata>
```

```
    <dc:title>My Book</dc:title>
    <dc:creator>John Doe</dc:creator>
    <dc:date>2024-04-30</dc:date>
  </metadata>
  <manifest>
    <item id="cover" href="cover.jpg" media-type="image/jpeg" />
    <item id="chapter1" href="chapter1.html" media-type="text/html" />
    <!-- Additional book content -->
  </manifest>
  <spine>
    <itemref idref="cover" />
    <itemref idref="chapter1" />
    <!-- Additional chapters -->
  </spine>
</package>
```

Use XML for Representing Bibliographic Information (MODS)

```
<!-- Example of using XML for representing bibliographic information (MODS) -->
<mods xmlns="http://www.loc.gov/mods/v3">
  <titleInfo>
    <title>My Book</title>
  </titleInfo>
  <name type="personal">
    <namePart>Doe, John</namePart>
  </name>
  <originInfo>
    <dateIssued>2024</dateIssued>
  </originInfo>
</mods>
```

Implement XML for Representing News Syndication (RSS/ATOM)

```xml
<!-- Example of using XML for representing news syndication (RSS/ATOM) -->
<rss version="2.0">
  <channel>
    <title>My News Feed</title>
    <link>http://www.example.com/news</link>
    <description>Latest news updates</description>
    <item>
      <title>Breaking News</title>
      <link>http://www.example.com/news/breaking</link>
      <description>Read about the breaking news</description>
    </item>
    <!-- Additional news items -->
  </channel>
</rss>
```

Use XML for Representing Genealogy Data (GEDCOM)

```xml
<!-- Example of using XML for representing genealogy data (GEDCOM) -->
<gedcom>
  <individual>
    <name>
      <given>John</given>
      <surname>Doe</surname>
    </name>
    <birth>
      <date>1980-01-15</date>
      <place>New York</place>
    </birth>
    <!-- Additional individual details -->
  </individual>
  <!-- Additional genealogy data -->
```

```
</gedcom>
```

Implement XML for Representing Multimedia Content (SVG)

```
<!-- Example of using XML for representing multimedia content (SVG) -->
<svg xmlns="http://www.w3.org/2000/svg" width="100" height="100">
  <circle cx="50" cy="50" r="40" stroke="black" stroke-width="2" fill="red" />
</svg>
```

Use XML for Representing Mathematical Formulas (MathML)

```
<!-- Example of using XML for representing mathematical formulas (MathML) -->
<math xmlns="http://www.w3.org/1998/Math/MathML">
  <mrow>
    <msup>
      <mi>x</mi>
      <mn>2</mn>
    </msup>
    <mo>+</mo>
    <mi>y</mi>
    <mo>=</mo>
    <mn>10</mn>
  </mrow>
</math>
```

Implement XML for Representing Geographic Data (GML)

```
<!-- Example of using XML for representing geographic data (GML) -->
<gml:Point xmlns:gml="http://www.opengis.net/gml">
  <gml:pos>51.5007 -0.1246</gml:pos>
</gml:Point>
```

Use XML for Representing Legal Documents (LegalXML)

```xml
<!-- Example of using XML for representing legal documents (LegalXML) -->
<legalDocument xmlns="http://www.example.com/legal">
  <title>Contract Agreement</title>
  <party>
    <name>ABC Corporation</name>
    <!-- Additional party details -->
  </party>
  <!-- Additional legal document content -->
</legalDocument>
```

Implement XML for Representing Educational Content (SCORM)

```xml
<!-- Example of using XML for representing educational content (SCORM) -->
<manifest xmlns="http://www.imsproject.org/xsd/imscp_rootv1p1p2"
xmlns:adlcp="http://www.adlnet.org/xsd/adlcp_rootv1p2"
xmlns:xsi="http://www.w3.org/2001/XMLSchema-instance">
  <metadata>
    <schema>ADL SCORM</schema>
    <!-- Additional metadata -->
  </metadata>
  <organizations>
    <organization identifier="org1">
      <title>My Course</title>
      <!-- Additional organization details -->
    </organization>
  </organizations>
  <!-- Additional content structure -->
</manifest>
```

Use XML for Representing Financial Data (XBRL)

```xml
<!-- Example of using XML for representing financial data (XBRL) -->
<xbrli:xbrl xmlns:xbrli="http://www.xbrl.org/2003/instance">
   <context id="CONTEXT1">
     <entity>
       <identifier scheme="http://www.sec.gov/CIK">0001234567</identifier>
     </entity>
     <period>
       <startDate>2024-01-01</startDate>
       <endDate>2024-12-31</endDate>
     </period>
     <!-- Additional context details -->
   </context>
   <fact contextRef="CONTEXT1" unitRef="USD" decimals="-3">1000000</fact>
   <!-- Additional financial data -->
</xbrli:xbrl>
```

Implement XML for Representing Project Data (MPX)

```xml
<!-- Example of using XML for representing project data (MPX) -->
<project xmlns="http://schemas.microsoft.com/project">
   <tasks>
     <task>
       <name>Task 1</name>
       <start>2024-04-30</start>
       <finish>2024-05-05</finish>
       <!-- Additional task details -->
     </task>
   </tasks>
   <!-- Additional project data -->
</project>
```

Use XML for Representing Web Services (WSDL)

```xml
<!-- Example of using XML for representing web services (WSDL) -->
<definitions xmlns="http://schemas.xmlsoap.org/wsdl/"
        xmlns:soap="http://schemas.xmlsoap.org/wsdl/soap/"
        xmlns:xsd="http://www.w3.org/2001/XMLSchema"
        name="MyWebService"
        targetNamespace="http://example.com/wsdl">
  <types>
    <xsd:schema>
      <!-- Define data types -->
    </xsd:schema>
  </types>
  <message name="RequestMessage">
    <!-- Define request message structure -->
  </message>
  <message name="ResponseMessage">
    <!-- Define response message structure -->
  </message>
  <portType name="MyWebServicePortType">
    <operation name="MyOperation">
      <input message="tns:RequestMessage"/>
      <output message="tns:ResponseMessage"/>
    </operation>
  </portType>
  <binding name="MyWebServiceBinding" type="tns:MyWebServicePortType">
    <soap:binding style="rpc" transport="http://schemas.xmlsoap.org/soap/http"/>
    <operation name="MyOperation">
      <soap:operation soapAction="http://example.com/MyOperation"/>
      <input>
        <soap:body use="encoded" namespace="http://example.com/wsdl"/>
      </input>
```

```
      <output>
         <soap:body use="encoded" namespace="http://example.com/wsdl"/>
      </output>
   </operation>
 </binding>
 <service name="MyWebService">
   <port name="MyWebServicePort" binding="tns:MyWebServiceBinding">
      <soap:address location="http://example.com/MyWebService"/>
   </port>
 </service>
</definitions>
```

Implement XML for Representing Business Processes (BPEL)

```
<!-- Example of using XML for representing business processes (BPEL) -->
<process xmlns="http://docs.oasis-open.org/wsbpel/2.0/process/executable"
      xmlns:tns="http://example.com/bpel"
      targetNamespace="http://example.com/bpel">
   <sequence>
     <receive partnerLink="client" operation="Operation1" variable="input"/>
     <invoke partnerLink="service1" operation="Operation2" inputVariable="input"
outputVariable="output"/>
     <reply partnerLink="client" operation="Operation1" variable="output"/>
   </sequence>
</process>
```

Use XML for Representing Healthcare Data (CDA)

```
<!-- Example of using XML for representing healthcare data (CDA) -->
<ClinicalDocument xmlns-"urn:hl7-org:v3">
   <title>Medical Record</title>
   <patient>
     <name>John Doe</name>
```

```
    <dob>1990-05-15</dob>
    <!-- Additional patient details -->
  </patient>
  <!-- Additional clinical data -->
</ClinicalDocument>
```

Implement XML for Representing Office Documents (OpenXML)

```
<!-- Example of using XML for representing office documents (OpenXML) -->
<document xmlns="http://schemas.openxmlformats.org/wordprocessingml/2006/main">
  <body>
    <p>Hello, world!</p>
    <!-- Additional document content -->
  </body>
</document>
```

Use XML for Representing Electronic Books (EPUB)

```
<!-- Example of using XML for representing electronic books (EPUB) -->
<package xmlns="http://www.idpf.org/2007/opf" unique-identifier="bookid">
  <metadata>
    <dc:title>My Book</dc:title>
    <dc:creator>John Doe</dc:creator>
    <dc:date>2024-04-30</dc:date>
  </metadata>
  <manifest>
    <item id="cover" href="cover.jpg" media-type="image/jpeg" />
    <item id="chapter1" href="chapter1.html" media-type="text/html" />
    <!-- Additional book content -->
  </manifest>
  <spine>
    <itemref idref="cover" />
    <itemref idref="chapter1" />
```

```
    <!-- Additional chapters -->
  </spine>
</package>
```

Implement XML for Representing Bibliographic Data (MARC)

```xml
<!-- Example of using XML for representing bibliographic data (MARC) -->
<record xmlns="http://www.loc.gov/MARC21/slim">
  <leader>01234cam a2200301 a 4500</leader>
  <controlfield tag="001">123456</controlfield>
  <datafield tag="245" ind1="0" ind2="0">
    <subfield code="a">My Book</subfield>
  </datafield>
  <!-- Additional bibliographic data -->
</record>
```

Use XML for Representing Calendar Data (iCalendar)

```xml
<!-- Example of using XML for representing calendar data (iCalendar) -->
<icalendar xmlns="urn:ietf:params:xml:ns:icalendar-2.0">
  <event>
    <summary>Meeting</summary>
    <location>Conference Room A</location>
    <start>2024-05-01T09:00:00</start>
    <end>2024-05-01T10:00:00</end>
    <!-- Additional event details -->
  </event>
</icalendar>
```

Implement XML for Representing Metadata (Dublin Core)

```xml
<!-- Example of using XML for representing metadata (Dublin Core) -->
<metadata xmlns:dc="http://purl.org/dc/elements/1.1/">
  <dc:title>Document Title</dc:title>
```

```xml
    <dc:creator>John Doe</dc:creator>
    <dc:date>2024-04-30</dc:date>
    <!-- Additional Dublin Core metadata elements -->
</metadata>
```

Use XML for Representing Social Network Data (FOAF)

```xml
<!-- Example of using XML for representing social network data (FOAF) -->
<foaf:Person xmlns:foaf="http://xmlns.com/foaf/0.1/">
    <foaf:name>John Doe</foaf:name>
    <foaf:knows>
      <foaf:Person>
        <foaf:name>Jane Smith</foaf:name>
      </foaf:Person>
    </foaf:knows>
    <!-- Additional FOAF data -->
</foaf:Person>
```

Implement XML for Representing E-learning Content (SCORM)

```xml
<!-- Example of using XML for representing e-learning content (SCORM) -->
<manifest xmlns="http://www.imsproject.org/xsd/imscp_rootv1p1p2"
xmlns:adlcp="http://www.adlnet.org/xsd/adlcp_rootv1p2"
xmlns:xsi="http://www.w3.org/2001/XMLSchema-instance">
    <metadata>
      <schema>ADL SCORM</schema>
      <!-- Additional metadata -->
    </metadata>
    <organizations>
      <organization identifier="org1">
        <title>My Course</title>
        <!-- Additional organization details -->
      </organization>
```

```
  </organizations>
  <!-- Additional content structure -->
</manifest>
```

Use XML for Representing Financial Transactions (OFX)

```
<!-- Example of using XML for representing financial transactions (OFX) -->
<OFX xmlns="http://www.ofx.net/schemas/2003/06">
  <SIGNONMSGSRSV1>
    <SONRS>
      <STATUS>
        <CODE>0</CODE>
        <SEVERITY>INFO</SEVERITY>
      </STATUS>
      <!-- Additional sign-on response details -->
    </SONRS>
  </SIGNONMSGSRSV1>
  <BANKMSGSRSV1>
    <STMTTRNRS>
      <TRNUID>12345</TRNUID>
      <!-- Additional statement transaction response -->
    </STMTTRNRS>
  </BANKMSGSRSV1>
</OFX>
```

Implement XML for Representing Project Management Data (MPX)

```
<!-- Example of using XML for representing project management data (MPX) -->
<project xmlns="http://schemas.microsoft.com/project">
  <tasks>
    <task>
      <name>Task 1</name>
      <start>2024-04-30</start>
```

```
      <finish>2024-05-05</finish>

        <!-- Additional task details -->

    </task>

  </tasks>

  <!-- Additional project data -->

</project>
```

Use XML for Representing Structured Documents (DocBook)

```
<!-- Example of using XML for representing structured documents (DocBook) -->

<article xmlns="http://docbook.org/ns/docbook">

  <title>Sample Document</title>

  <section>

    <title>Introduction</title>

    <para>This is a sample document.</para>

  </section>

  <!-- Additional document sections -->

</article>
```

Implement XML for Representing Syndicated Web Content (RDF)

```
<!-- Example of using XML for representing syndicated web content (RDF) -->

<rdf:RDF xmlns:rdf="http://www.w3.org/1999/02/22-rdf-syntax-ns#"

      xmlns:dc="http://purl.org/dc/elements/1.1/">

  <rdf:Description rdf:about="http://example.com/article">

    <dc:title>Sample Article</dc:title>

    <dc:creator>John Doe</dc:creator>

    <dc:date>2024-04-30</dc:date>

    <!-- Additional RDF metadata -->

  </rdf:Description>

</rdf:RDF>
```

Use XML for Representing Remote Procedure Calls (XML-RPC)

```
<!-- Example of using XML for representing remote procedure calls (XML-RPC) -->
<methodCall>
  <methodName>sum</methodName>
  <params>
    <param>
      <value><int>5</int></value>
    </param>
    <param>
      <value><int>10</int></value>
    </param>
  </params>
</methodCall>
```

Implement XML for Representing Mathematical Markup (MathML)

```
<!-- Example of using XML for representing mathematical markup (MathML) -->
<math xmlns="http://www.w3.org/1998/Math/MathML">
  <mrow>
    <msup>
      <mi>x</mi>
      <mn>2</mn>
    </msup>
    <mo>+</mo>
    <mi>y</mi>
    <mo>=</mo>
    <mn>10</mn>
  </mrow>
</math>
```

Use XML for Representing Chemical Data (CML)

```xml
<!-- Example of using XML for representing chemical data (CML) -->
<cml xmlns="http://www.xml-cml.org/schema">
  <molecule title="Water">
    <atomArray>
      <atom id="a1" elementType="O" x3="0.0" y3="0.0" z3="0.0" />
      <atom id="a2" elementType="H" x3="0.757" y3="0.586" z3="0.0" />
      <atom id="a3" elementType="H" x3="-0.757" y3="0.586" z3="0.0" />
      <!-- Additional atoms and bonds -->
    </atomArray>
  </molecule>
</cml>
```

Implement XML for Representing GIS Data (GML)

```xml
<!-- Example of using XML for representing GIS data (GML) -->
<gml:Point xmlns:gml="http://www.opengis.net/gml">
  <gml:pos>51.5007 -0.1246</gml:pos>
</gml:Point>
```

Use XML for Representing E-commerce Transactions (UBL)

```xml
<!-- Example of using XML for representing e-commerce transactions (UBL) -->
<Invoice xmlns="urn:oasis:names:specification:ubl:schema:xsd:Invoice-2"

xmlns:cac="urn:oasis:names:specification:ubl:schema:xsd:CommonAggregateComponents-2">
  <ID>123456</ID>
  <IssueDate>2024-04-30</IssueDate>
  <AccountingSupplierParty>
    <Party>
      <PartyName>XYZ Corporation</PartyName>
      <!-- Additional supplier details -->
```

```
    </Party>

  </AccountingSupplierParty>

  <!-- Additional invoice data -->

</Invoice>
```

Implement XML for Representing Multimedia Presentations (SMIL)

```
<!-- Example of using XML for representing multimedia presentations (SMIL) -->

<smil xmlns="http://www.w3.org/2001/SMIL20/Language">

  <body>

    <par>

      <img src="image1.jpg" />

      <text src="text1.txt" />

      <!-- Additional multimedia elements -->

    </par>

  </body>

</smil>
```

Use XML for Representing User Interfaces (XUL)

```
<!-- Example of using XML for representing user interfaces (XUL) -->

<?xml version="1.0"?>

<window xmlns="http://www.mozilla.org/keymaster/gatekeeper/there.is.only.xul"

    title="My Application" width="400" height="300">

  <vbox>

    <label value="Welcome to My Application!" />

    <button label="Click Me" oncommand="alert('Button clicked!');" />

  </vbox>

</window>
```

Implement XML for Representing Digital Books (EPUB)

```
<!-- Example of using XML for representing digital books (EPUB) -->

<package xmlns="http://www.idpf.org/2007/opf" unique-identifier="bookid">
```

```xml
  <metadata>
    <dc:title>My Book</dc:title>
    <dc:creator>John Doe</dc:creator>
    <dc:date>2024-04-30</dc:date>
  </metadata>
  <manifest>
    <item id="cover" href="cover.jpg" media-type="image/jpeg" />
    <item id="chapter1" href="chapter1.html" media-type="text/html" />
    <!-- Additional book content -->
  </manifest>
  <spine>
    <itemref idref="cover" />
    <itemref idref="chapter1" />
    <!-- Additional chapters -->
  </spine>
</package>
```

Use XML for Representing Bibliographic Information (MODS)

```xml
<!-- Example of using XML for representing bibliographic information (MODS) -->
<mods xmlns="http://www.loc.gov/mods/v3">
  <titleInfo>
    <title>My Book</title>
  </titleInfo>
  <name type="personal">
    <namePart>Doe, John</namePart>
  </name>
  <originInfo>
    <dateIssued>2024</dateIssued>
  </originInfo>
</mods>
```

Implement XML for Representing News Syndication (RSS/ATOM)

```xml
<!-- Example of using XML for representing news syndication (RSS/ATOM) -->
<rss version="2.0" xmlns:atom="http://www.w3.org/2005/Atom">
  <channel>
    <title>News Feed</title>
    <link>http://example.com/news</link>
    <description>Latest news updates</description>
    <item>
      <title>Breaking News</title>
      <link>http://example.com/news/article1</link>
      <description>Details of breaking news</description>
      <pubDate>2024-04-30T12:00:00</pubDate>
    </item>
    <!-- Additional news items -->
  </channel>
</rss>
```

Use XML for Representing Genealogy Data (GEDCOM)

```xml
<!-- Example of using XML for representing genealogy data (GEDCOM) -->
<gedcom>
  <individual>
    <name>
      <given>John</given>
      <surname>Doe</surname>
    </name>
    <birth>
      <date>1980-01-15</date>
      <place>New York</place>
    </birth>
    <!-- Additional individual details -->
```

```
  </individual>

  <!-- Additional genealogy data -->

</gedcom>
```

Implement XML for Representing Multimedia Content (SVG)

```
<!-- Example of using XML for representing multimedia content (SVG) -->

<svg xmlns="http://www.w3.org/2000/svg" width="100" height="100">

  <circle cx="50" cy="50" r="40" stroke="black" stroke-width="2" fill="red" />

</svg>
```

Use XML for Representing Mathematical Formulas (MathML)

```
<!-- Example of using XML for representing mathematical formulas (MathML) -->

<math xmlns="http://www.w3.org/1998/Math/MathML">

  <mrow>

    <msup>

      <mi>x</mi>

      <mn>2</mn>

    </msup>

    <mo>+</mo>

    <mi>y</mi>

    <mo>=</mo>

    <mn>10</mn>

  </mrow>

</math>
```

Implement XML for Representing Geographic Data (GML)

```
<!-- Example of using XML for representing geographic data (GML) -->

<gml:Point xmlns:gml="http://www.opengis.net/gml">

  <gml:pos>51.5007 -0.1246</gml:pos>

</gml:Point>
```

Use XML for Representing Legal Documents (LegalXML)

```
<!-- Example of using XML for representing legal documents (LegalXML) -->
<legalDocument xmlns="http://www.example.com/legal">
  <title>Contract Agreement</title>
  <party>
    <name>ABC Corporation</name>
    <!-- Additional party details -->
  </party>
  <!-- Additional legal document content -->
</legalDocument>
```

Implement XML for Representing Educational Content (SCORM)

```
<!-- Example of using XML for representing educational content (SCORM) -->
<manifest xmlns="http://www.imsproject.org/xsd/imscp_rootv1p1p2"
xmlns:adlcp="http://www.adlnet.org/xsd/adlcp_rootv1p2"
xmlns:xsi="http://www.w3.org/2001/XMLSchema-instance">
  <metadata>
    <schema>ADL SCORM</schema>
    <!-- Additional metadata -->
  </metadata>
  <organizations>
    <organization identifier="org1">
      <title>My Course</title>
      <!-- Additional organization details -->
    </organization>
  </organizations>
  <!-- Additional content structure -->
</manifest>
```

Use XML for Representing Financial Data (XBRL)

```xml
<!-- Example of using XML for representing financial data (XBRL) -->
<xbrli:xbrl xmlns:xbrli="http://www.xbrl.org/2003/instance">
   <context id="CONTEXT1">
      <entity>
         <identifier scheme="http://www.sec.gov/CIK">0001234567</identifier>
      </entity>
      <period>
         <startDate>2024-01-01</startDate>
         <endDate>2024-12-31</endDate>
      </period>
      <!-- Additional context details -->
   </context>
   <fact contextRef="CONTEXT1" unitRef="USD" decimals="-3">1000000</fact>
   <!-- Additional financial data -->
</xbrli:xbrl>
```

Implement XML for Representing Project Data (MPX)

```xml
<!-- Example of using XML for representing project data (MPX) -->
<project xmlns="http://schemas.microsoft.com/project">
   <tasks>
      <task>
         <name>Task 1</name>
         <start>2024-04-30</start>
         <finish>2024-05-05</finish>
         <!-- Additional task details -->
      </task>
   </tasks>
   <!-- Additional project data -->
</project>
```

Use XML for Representing Web Services (WSDL)

```xml
<!-- Example of using XML for representing web services (WSDL) -->
<definitions xmlns="http://schemas.xmlsoap.org/wsdl/"
        xmlns:soap="http://schemas.xmlsoap.org/wsdl/soap/"
        xmlns:xsd="http://www.w3.org/2001/XMLSchema"
        name="MyWebService"
        targetNamespace="http://example.com/wsdl">
  <types>
    <xsd:schema>
      <!-- Define data types -->
    </xsd:schema>
  </types>
  <message name="RequestMessage">
    <!-- Define request message -->
  </message>
  <message name="ResponseMessage">
    <!-- Define response message -->
  </message>
  <portType name="MyWebServicePortType">
    <!-- Define port type -->
  </portType>
  <binding name="MyWebServiceBinding" type="tns:MyWebServicePortType">
    <soap:binding style="document" transport="http://schemas.xmlsoap.org/soap/http"
/>
    <!-- Define binding details -->
  </binding>
  <service name="MyWebService">
    <port name="MyWebServicePort" binding="tns:MyWebServiceBinding">
      <soap:address location="http://example.com/service" />
    </port>
  </service>
```

```
</definitions>
```

Implement XML for Representing Business Processes (BPEL)

```
<!-- Example of using XML for representing business processes (BPEL) -->
<process xmlns="http://docs.oasis-open.org/wsbpel/2.0/process/executable"
      xmlns:tns="http://example.com/bpel"
      targetNamespace="http://example.com/bpel"
      name="MyProcess">
  <sequence>
    <receive inputVariable="inputVariable1" operation="operation1" />
    <assign>
      <copy>
        <from expression="inputVariable1.payload" />
        <to variable="variable1" />
      </copy>
    </assign>
    <invoke partnerLink="partnerLink1" operation="operation2" />
    <!-- Additional process steps -->
  </sequence>
</process>
```

Use XML for Representing Healthcare Data (CDA)

```
<!-- Example of using XML for representing healthcare data (CDA) -->
<ClinicalDocument xmlns="urn:hl7-org:v3">
  <id root="1.2.3.4.5" />
  <title>Health Record</title>
  <patient>
    <name>John Doe</name>
    <birthdate>1980-01-15</birthdate>
    <!-- Additional patient information -->
  </patient>
```

```xml
    <!-- Additional clinical data -->
</ClinicalDocument>
```

Implement XML for Representing Office Documents (OpenXML)

```xml
<!-- Example of using XML for representing office documents (OpenXML) -->
<document xmlns="http://schemas.openxmlformats.org/wordprocessingml/2006/main">
  <body>
    <p>Hello, world!</p>
    <!-- Additional document content -->
  </body>
</document>
```

Use XML for Representing Electronic Books (EPUB)

```xml
<!-- Example of using XML for representing electronic books (EPUB) -->
<package xmlns="http://www.idpf.org/2007/opf" unique-identifier="bookid">
  <metadata>
    <dc:title>My Book</dc:title>
    <dc:creator>John Doe</dc:creator>
    <dc:date>2024-04-30</dc:date>
  </metadata>
  <manifest>
    <item id="cover" href="cover.jpg" media-type="image/jpeg" />
    <item id="chapter1" href="chapter1.html" media-type="text/html" />
    <!-- Additional book content -->
  </manifest>
  <spine>
    <itemref idref="cover" />
    <itemref idref="chapter1" />
    <!-- Additional chapters -->
  </spine>
</package>
```

Implement XML for Representing Bibliographic Data (MARC)

```xml
<!-- Example of using XML for representing bibliographic data (MARC) -->
<record xmlns="http://www.loc.gov/MARC21/slim">
  <leader>01234cam a2200301 a 4500</leader>
  <controlfield tag="001">123456</controlfield>
  <datafield tag="245" ind1="0" ind2="0">
    <subfield code="a">My Book</subfield>
  </datafield>
  <!-- Additional bibliographic data -->
</record>
```

Use XML for Representing Calendar Data (iCalendar)

```xml
<!-- Example of using XML for representing calendar data (iCalendar) -->
<icalendar xmlns="urn:ietf:params:xml:ns:icalendar-2.0">
  <event>
    <summary>Meeting</summary>
    <location>Conference Room A</location>
    <start>2024-05-01T09:00:00</start>
    <end>2024-05-01T10:00:00</end>
    <!-- Additional event details -->
  </event>
</icalendar>
```

Implement XML for Representing Metadata (Dublin Core)

```xml
<!-- Example of using XML for representing metadata (Dublin Core) -->
<metadata xmlns:dc="http://purl.org/dc/elements/1.1/">
  <dc:title>Document Title</dc:title>
  <dc:creator>John Doe</dc:creator>
  <dc:date>2024-04-30</dc:date>
  <!-- Additional Dublin Core metadata elements -->
</metadata>
```

Use XML for Representing Social Network Data (FOAF)

```xml
<!-- Example of using XML for representing social network data (FOAF) -->
<foaf:Person xmlns:foaf="http://xmlns.com/foaf/0.1/">
  <foaf:name>John Doe</foaf:name>
  <foaf:knows>
    <foaf:Person>
      <foaf:name>Jane Smith</foaf:name>
    </foaf:Person>
  </foaf:knows>
  <!-- Additional FOAF data -->
</foaf:Person>
```

Implement XML for Representing E-learning Content (SCORM)

```xml
<!-- Example of using XML for representing e-learning content (SCORM) -->
<manifest xmlns="http://www.imsproject.org/xsd/imscp_rootv1p1p2"
xmlns:adlcp="http://www.adlnet.org/xsd/adlcp_rootv1p2"
xmlns:xsi="http://www.w3.org/2001/XMLSchema-instance">
  <metadata>
    <schema>ADL SCORM</schema>
    <!-- Additional metadata -->
  </metadata>
  <organizations>
    <organization identifier="org1">
      <title>My Course</title>
      <!-- Additional organization details -->
    </organization>
  </organizations>
  <!-- Additional content structure -->
</manifest>
```

Use XML for Representing Financial Transactions (OFX)

```xml
<!-- Example of using XML for representing financial transactions (OFX) -->
<OFX>
  <SIGNONMSGSRSV1>
    <SONRS>
      <STATUS>
        <CODE>0</CODE>
        <SEVERITY>INFO</SEVERITY>
      </STATUS>
      <!-- Additional sign-on response details -->
    </SONRS>
  </SIGNONMSGSRSV1>
  <!-- Additional OFX data -->
</OFX>
```

Implement XML for Representing Business Processes (BPEL)

```xml
<!-- Example of using XML for representing business processes (BPEL) -->
<process xmlns="http://docs.oasis-open.org/wsbpel/2.0/process/executable"
    xmlns:tns="http://example.com/bpel"
    targetNamespace="http://example.com/bpel"
    name="MyProcess">
  <sequence>
    <receive inputVariable="inputVariable1" operation="operation1" />
    <assign>
      <copy>
        <from expression="inputVariable1.payload" />
        <to variable="variable1" />
      </copy>
    </assign>
    <invoke partnerLink="partnerLink1" operation="operation2" />
    <!-- Additional process steps -->
```

```xml
  </sequence>

</process>
```

Use XML for Representing Healthcare Data (CDA)

```xml
<!-- Example of using XML for representing healthcare data (CDA) -->
<ClinicalDocument xmlns="urn:hl7-org:v3">
  <id root="1.2.3.4.5" />
  <title>Health Record</title>
  <patient>
    <name>John Doe</name>
    <birthdate>1980-01-15</birthdate>
    <!-- Additional patient information -->
  </patient>
  <!-- Additional clinical data -->
</ClinicalDocument>
```

Implement XML for Representing Office Documents (OpenXML)

```xml
<!-- Example of using XML for representing office documents (OpenXML) -->
<document xmlns="http://schemas.openxmlformats.org/wordprocessingml/2006/main">
  <body>
    <p>Hello, world!</p>
    <!-- Additional document content -->
  </body>
</document>
```

Use XML for Representing Electronic Books (EPUB)

```xml
<!-- Example of using XML for representing electronic books (EPUB) -->
<package xmlns="http://www.idpf.org/2007/opf" unique-identifier="bookid">
  <metadata>
    <dc:title>My Book</dc:title>
    <dc:creator>John Doe</dc:creator>
```

```
      <dc:date>2024-04-30</dc:date>
   </metadata>
   <manifest>
      <item id="cover" href="cover.jpg" media-type="image/jpeg" />
      <item id="chapter1" href="chapter1.html" media-type="text/html" />
      <!-- Additional book content -->
   </manifest>
   <spine>
      <itemref idref="cover" />
      <itemref idref="chapter1" />
      <!-- Additional chapters -->
   </spine>
</package>
```

Implement XML for Representing Bibliographic Data (MARC)

```
<!-- Example of using XML for representing bibliographic data (MARC) -->
<record xmlns="http://www.loc.gov/MARC21/slim">
   <leader>01234cam a2200301 a 4500</leader>
   <controlfield tag="001">123456</controlfield>
   <datafield tag="245" ind1="0" ind2="0">
      <subfield code="a">My Book</subfield>
   </datafield>
   <!-- Additional bibliographic data -->
</record>
```

Use XML for Representing Calendar Data (iCalendar)

```
<!-- Example of using XML for representing calendar data (iCalendar) -->
<icalendar xmlns="urn:ietf:params:xml:ns:icalendar-2.0">
   <event>
      <summary>Meeting</summary>
      <location>Conference Room A</location>
```

```
    <start>2024-05-01T09:00:00</start>

    <end>2024-05-01T10:00:00</end>

    <!-- Additional event details -->

  </event>

</icalendar>
```

Implement XML for Representing Metadata (Dublin Core)

```
<!-- Example of using XML for representing metadata (Dublin Core) -->

<metadata xmlns:dc="http://purl.org/dc/elements/1.1/">

  <dc:title>Document Title</dc:title>

  <dc:creator>John Doe</dc:creator>

  <dc:date>2024-04-30</dc:date>

  <!-- Additional Dublin Core metadata elements -->

</metadata>
```

Use XML for Representing Social Network Data (FOAF)

```
<!-- Example of using XML for representing social network data (FOAF) -->

<foaf:Person xmlns:foaf="http://xmlns.com/foaf/0.1/">

  <foaf:name>John Doe</foaf:name>

  <foaf:knows>

    <foaf:Person>

      <foaf:name>Jane Smith</foaf:name>

    </foaf:Person>

  </foaf:knows>

  <!-- Additional FOAF data -->

</foaf:Person>
```

Implement XML for Representing E-learning Content (SCORM)

```xml
<!-- Example of using XML for representing e-learning content (SCORM) -->
<manifest xmlns="http://www.imsproject.org/xsd/imscp_rootv1p1p2"
xmlns:adlcp="http://www.adlnet.org/xsd/adlcp_rootv1p2"
xmlns:xsi="http://www.w3.org/2001/XMLSchema-instance">
  <metadata>
    <schema>ADL SCORM</schema>
    <!-- Additional metadata -->
  </metadata>
  <organizations>
    <organization identifier="org1">
      <title>My Course</title>
      <!-- Additional organization details -->
    </organization>
  </organizations>
  <!-- Additional content structure -->
</manifest>
```

Use XML for Representing Financial Transactions (OFX)

```xml
<!-- Example of using XML for representing financial transactions (OFX) -->
<OFX>
  <SIGNONMSGSRSV1>
    <SONRS>
      <STATUS>
        <CODE>0</CODE>
        <SEVERITY>INFO</SEVERITY>
      </STATUS>
      <!-- Additional sign-on response details -->
    </SONRS>
  </SIGNONMSGSRSV1>
  <!-- Additional OFX data -->
```

```
</OFX>
```

Implement XML for Representing Project Management Data (MPX)

```
<!-- Example of using XML for representing project management data (MPX) -->
<project xmlns="http://schemas.microsoft.com/project">
    <tasks>
        <task>
            <name>Task 1</name>
            <start>2024-04-30</start>
            <finish>2024-05-05</finish>
            <!-- Additional task details -->
        </task>
    </tasks>
    <!-- Additional project data -->
</project>
```

Use XML for Representing Structured Documents (DocBook)

```
<!-- Example of using XML for representing structured documents (DocBook) -->
<article xmlns="http://docbook.org/ns/docbook">
    <title>Sample Document</title>
    <section>
        <title>Introduction</title>
        <para>This is the introduction section.</para>
    </section>
    <!-- Additional sections and content -->
</article>
```

Implement XML for Representing Syndicated Web Content (RDF)

```
<!-- Example of using XML for representing syndicated web content (RDF) -->
<rdf:RDF xmlns:rdf="http://www.w3.org/1999/02/22-rdf-syntax-ns#"
        xmlns:dc="http://purl.org/dc/elements/1.1/">
```

```
<rdf:Description rdf:about="http://example.com/article1">
    <dc:title>Article 1</dc:title>
    <dc:description>This is article 1.</dc:description>
  </rdf:Description>
  <!-- Additional RDF triples -->
</rdf:RDF>
```

Use XML for Representing Remote Procedure Calls (XML-RPC)

```
<!-- Example of using XML for representing remote procedure calls (XML-RPC) -->
<methodCall>
  <methodName>exampleMethod</methodName>
  <params>
    <param>
      <value><string>param1</string></value>
    </param>
    <!-- Additional parameters -->
  </params>
</methodCall>
```

Implement XML for Representing Mathematical Markup (MathML)

```
<!-- Example of using XML for representing mathematical markup (MathML) -->
<math xmlns="http://www.w3.org/1998/Math/MathML">
  <mrow>
    <msup>
      <mi>x</mi>
      <mn>2</mn>
    </msup>
    <mo>+</mo>
    <mi>y</mi>
    <mo>=</mo>
    <mn>10</mn>
```

```
  </mrow>
</math>
```

Use XML for Representing Chemical Data (CML)

```
<!-- Example of using XML for representing chemical data (CML) -->
<chemical xmlns="http://example.com/chemical">
  <compound>
    <name>Water</name>
    <formula>H2O</formula>
  </compound>
  <!-- Additional chemical data -->
</chemical>
```

Implement XML for Representing GIS Data (GML)

```
<!-- Example of using XML for representing GIS data (GML) -->
<gml:Point xmlns:gml="http://www.opengis.net/gml">
  <gml:pos>51.5007 -0.1246</gml:pos>
</gml:Point>
```

Use XML for Representing E-commerce Transactions (UBL)

```
<!-- Example of using XML for representing e-commerce transactions (UBL) -->
<Invoice xmlns="urn:oasis:names:specification:ubl:schema:xsd:Invoice-2"

xmlns:cac="urn:oasis:names:specification:ubl:schema:xsd:CommonAggregateCompone
nts-2">
  <cac:AccountingSupplierParty>
    <!-- Supplier details -->
  </cac:AccountingSupplierParty>
  <cac:AccountingCustomerParty>
    <!-- Customer details -->
  </cac:AccountingCustomerParty>
```

```
  <!-- Additional invoice details -->
</Invoice>
```

Implement XML for Representing Multimedia Presentations (SMIL)

```
<!-- Example of using XML for representing multimedia presentations (SMIL) -->
<smil xmlns="http://www.w3.org/ns/SMIL">
  <head>
    <layout>
      <root-layout width="800px" height="600px" />
    </layout>
  </head>
  <body>
    <par>
      <img src="image1.jpg" region="main" />
      <text src="text1.txt" region="sidebar" />
    </par>
  </body>
</smil>
```

Use XML for Representing User Interfaces (XUL)

```
<!-- Example of using XML for representing user interfaces (XUL) -->
<window xmlns="http://www.mozilla.org/keymaster/gatekeeper/there.is.only.xul">
  <button label="Click Me" />
  <textbox value="Hello, world!" />
  <!-- Additional user interface elements -->
</window>
```

Implement XML for Representing Digital Books (EPUB)

```
<!-- Example of using XML for representing digital books (EPUB) -->
<package xmlns="http://www.idpf.org/2007/opf" unique-identifier="bookid">
  <metadata>
```

```xml
      <dc:title>My Book</dc:title>
      <dc:creator>John Doe</dc:creator>
      <dc:date>2024-04-30</dc:date>
   </metadata>
   <manifest>
      <item id="cover" href="cover.jpg" media-type="image/jpeg" />
      <item id="chapter1" href="chapter1.html" media-type="text/html" />
      <!-- Additional book content -->
   </manifest>
   <spine>
      <itemref idref="cover" />
      <itemref idref="chapter1" />
      <!-- Additional chapters -->
   </spine>
</package>
```

Use XML for Representing Bibliographic Information (MODS)

```xml
<!-- Example of using XML for representing bibliographic information (MODS) -->
<mods xmlns="http://www.loc.gov/mods/v3">
   <titleInfo>
      <title>Sample Title</title>
   </titleInfo>
   <name>
      <namePart>John Doe</namePart>
      <role>
         <roleTerm type="text">Author</roleTerm>
      </role>
   </name>
   <!-- Additional bibliographic details -->
</mods>
```

Implement XML for Representing News Syndication (RSS/ATOM)

```xml
<!-- Example of using XML for representing news syndication (RSS/ATOM) -->
<rss xmlns:atom="http://www.w3.org/2005/Atom" version="2.0">
  <channel>
    <title>News Feed</title>
    <link>http://example.com</link>
    <description>Latest news updates</description>
    <item>
      <title>Breaking News</title>
      <link>http://example.com/news1</link>
      <description>Details of breaking news</description>
    </item>
    <!-- Additional news items -->
  </channel>
</rss>
```

Use XML for Representing Genealogy Data (GEDCOM)

```xml
<!-- Example of using XML for representing genealogy data (GEDCOM) -->
<gedcom>
  <individual>
    <name>John Doe</name>
    <birthdate>1980-01-15</birthdate>
    <!-- Additional individual information -->
  </individual>
  <!-- Additional genealogy data -->
</gedcom>
```

Implement XML for Representing Multimedia Content (SVG)

```xml
<!-- Example of using XML for representing multimedia content (SVG) -->
<svg xmlns="http://www.w3.org/2000/svg" width="400" height="400">
  <rect x="50" y="50" width="300" height="300" fill="blue" />
```

```
    <circle cx="200" cy="200" r="100" fill="yellow" />

    <!-- Additional SVG shapes and content -->

</svg>
```

Use XML for Representing Mathematical Formulas (MathML)

```
<!-- Example of using XML for representing mathematical formulas (MathML) -->

<math xmlns="http://www.w3.org/1998/Math/MathML">

    <mrow>

      <msup>

        <mi>x</mi>

        <mn>2</mn>

      </msup>

      <mo>+</mo>

      <mi>y</mi>

      <mo>=</mo>

      <mn>10</mn>

    </mrow>

</math>
```

Implement XML for Representing Geographic Data (GML)

```
<!-- Example of using XML for representing geographic data (GML) -->

<gml:Point xmlns:gml="http://www.opengis.net/gml">

    <gml:pos>51.5007 -0.1246</gml:pos>

</gml:Point>
```

Use XML for Representing Legal Documents (LegalXML)

```
<!-- Example of using XML for representing legal documents (LegalXML) -->

<legalDocument xmlns="http://example.com/legal">

    <title>Legal Agreement</title>

    <party role="issuer">John Doe</party>

    <party role="recipient">Jane Smith</party>
```

```xml
  <!-- Additional legal document details -->
</legalDocument>
```

Implement XML for Representing Educational Content (SCORM)

```xml
<!-- Example of using XML for representing educational content (SCORM) -->
<manifest xmlns="http://www.imsproject.org/xsd/imscp_rootv1p1p2"
xmlns:adlcp="http://www.adlnet.org/xsd/adlcp_rootv1p2"
xmlns:xsi="http://www.w3.org/2001/XMLSchema-instance">
  <metadata>
    <schema>ADL SCORM</schema>
    <!-- Additional metadata -->
  </metadata>
  <organizations>
    <organization identifier="org1">
      <title>My Course</title>
      <!-- Additional organization details -->
    </organization>
  </organizations>
  <!-- Additional content structure -->
</manifest>
```

Use XML for Representing Financial Data (XBRL)

```xml
<!-- Example of using XML for representing financial data (XBRL) -->
<xbrl xmlns="http://www.xbrl.org/2003/instance">
  <context>
    <entity>
      <identifier scheme="http://www.sec.gov/cik">0001234567</identifier>
    </entity>
    <period>
      <startDate>2024-01-01</startDate>
      <endDate>2024-12-31</endDate>
```

```
      </period>
   </context>
   <facts>
      <fact name="Revenues" value="1000000" />
      <!-- Additional financial facts -->
   </facts>
</xbrl>
```

Implement XML for Representing Project Data (MPX)

```
<!-- Example of using XML for representing project data (MPX) -->
<project xmlns="http://schemas.microsoft.com/project">
   <tasks>
      <task>
         <name>Task 1</name>
         <start>2024-04-30</start>
         <finish>2024-05-05</finish>
         <!-- Additional task details -->
      </task>
   </tasks>
   <!-- Additional project data -->
</project>
```

Use XML for Representing Web Services (WSDL)

```
<!-- Example of using XML for representing web services (WSDL) -->
<definitions xmlns="http://schemas.xmlsoap.org/wsdl/"
        xmlns:tns="http://example.com/service"
        targetNamespace="http://example.com/service">
   <service name="MyService">
      <port name="MyPort" binding="tns:MyBinding">
         <soap:address location="http://example.com/service" />
      </port>
```

```
  </service>

  <!-- Additional service definitions -->
</definitions>
```

Implement XML for Representing Business Processes (BPEL)

```
<!-- Example of using XML for representing business processes (BPEL) -->
<process xmlns="http://docs.oasis-open.org/wsbpel/2.0/process/executable"
    xmlns:tns="http://example.com/bpel"
    targetNamespace="http://example.com/bpel"
    name="MyProcess">
  <sequence>
    <receive inputVariable="inputVariable1" operation="operation1" />
    <assign>
      <copy>
        <from expression="inputVariable1.payload" />
        <to variable="variable1" />
      </copy>
    </assign>
    <invoke partnerLink="partnerLink1" operation="operation2" />
    <!-- Additional process steps -->
  </sequence>
</process>
```

9 789334 060379